RealLivePreacher.com

RealLivePreacher.com

GORDON ATKINSON

WILLIAM B. EERDMANS PUBLISHING COMPANY
GRAND RAPIDS, MICHIGAN / CAMBRIDGE, U.K.

© 2004 Wm. B. Eerdmans Publishing Co.

Wm. B. Eerdmans Publishing Co.
255 Jefferson Ave. S.E., Grand Rapids, Michigan 49503 /
P.O. Box 163, Cambridge CB3 9PU U.K.
www.eerdmans.com

Printed in the United States of America

09 08 07 06 05 04   7 6 5 4 3 2 1

Library of Congress Cataloging-in-Publication Data

Atkinson, Gordon, 1961-
    Reallivepreacher.com / Gordon Atkinson.
        p.   cm.
    ISBN 0-8028-2810-8 (pbk. alk. paper)
    I. Christianity — Miscellanea.   I. Title: Real live preacher.com   II. Title.

    BR124.A85   2004
    242 — dc22

                                                    2004056310

The artwork in this volume was created by Steve Erspamer
and is taken from *Religious Clip Art for the Liturgical Year.*
It is used by permission of Liturgical Training Publications.

Contents

Foreword

Most of this book originally appeared as postings to a weblog called "Real Live Preacher." This frequently updated Internet journal began appearing in late 2002 and was an immediate sensation. The anonymous Preacher's observations about his life as a working minister in a small Texas congregation fascinated religious and secular readers all over the world.

A collection of weblog posts is like an album of live improvised music. Reading the same material in a book isn't the same experience as watching it appear on a weblog over time — the "live" in the Real Live Preacher. You, reader, hold in your hand concrete proof that installments kept appearing in large numbers. We didn't have that — indeed, we would have been happy for a half dozen or a dozen postings — but what we got was to see the unfolding of the Preacher in time.

And over time, we encouraged him. Many of us linked to him from our own weblogs, sending fresh waves of curious readers his way. His comment section began to overflow with remarks from visitors — encouragement, criticism, arguments among themselves. What had begun as the Preacher's own platform had become a social space, a community, a destination for a whole distinctive crew. It still is.

Only writers fantasize about the lives of editors, but everyone who's ever been to a religious service has probably wondered what it's like to be the preacher. The Real Live Preacher takes us through that door and into the surprising world behind it — a world of mundane and yet startling details (religious tat supply companies!), of worry about the everyday lives of his parishioners, a world in which Sunday is the hardest-working day of his week, a world in which the cosmic and the everyday hash it out, just like in everybody else's life.

Among other things, the Preacher reminds us what it's like to be the one member of the congregation who doesn't have the Preacher to fall back on. George Harrison once remarked that he and the three other guys were the only people to go through the 1960s without the Beatles. It's kind of like that. The Preacher copes — badly sometimes, wonderfully at other times, full of self-doubt and stumbling and acutely aware that being good with words doesn't make you right. "My sin is having words that are far more beautiful than my life." But they're good words and they nourish a lot of other lives.

What do we learn from the Real Live Preacher? Nothing that will make headlines in the *New York Times*. We learn things that we already knew. That great truths tend to be simple, but putting them into practice is hard. That religion isn't a set of positions, but rather something that gets done. And that "God is in the details" isn't just a figure of speech.

PATRICK NIELSEN HAYDEN
http://nielsenhayden.com/electrolite

Preface

In the fall of 2002 I stumbled across the Salon.com weblog community, having no idea what a weblog was. I was immediately captivated by this new thing I had found. Here were regular people, just like me, writing and posting their work online. There were personal journals with tantalizing peeks into other people's lives, political analysts, storytellers, complainers, exhibitionists, and more. Some of the writing was rough and some was beautiful, but the quality of the work seemed less important to me than the idea of what they were doing.

They were writing as honestly as they could and putting their words online for the whole world to see.

"Anyone can do this?" I said out loud. "Anyone can just write whatever they want and put it online in one of these weblogs?"

For two months I read blogs at night and considered this new medium. At that time my own creative energy was being poured into sermons and other writing that I did for the church, but I was feeling a strong desire to express myself in a new way. I began to fantasize about starting my own weblog.

I am the pastor of a church. In the context of that calling, I must always consider how people will receive what I write and say. As one of the shepherds of our flock, I am responsible for the telling, but also for walking with people as they hear and respond. This responsibility weighs heavily on me at times.

I wanted to write. I wanted only to write. I wanted to gather my best words and thoughts together and present them to the world. I wanted to be free from the worry and responsibility of considering how people might react to my writing. It seemed to me that a weblog would be a perfect way to make this fantasy become a reality.

Impulsively, I downloaded the software needed to launch a weblog and vowed to give it a try. I decided I would remain anonymous, which I felt would give me the freedom to write honestly without worrying about how people in my church might react.

The software required that my blog be given a title. I sat at my computer for a few minutes, staring at the screen. Suddenly I had a funny image in my mind of a sideshow barker shouting, "Come, see a real live preacher!" I laughed and typed "Real Live Preacher" into the appropriate slot. I wrote my first entry, posting it on December 6, 2002.

I found my style by my third posting, which was called "Earl the Grave Digger." I quickly settled into writing carefully crafted essays. Many bloggers keep a kind of online journal, posting something every day. I wanted to put a lot of work into my writing, so I decided to post only two or three times a week. Even so, this was a huge commitment to make. I had no idea what I was getting myself into.

The title of my blog brought immediate attention. Some of the Salon bloggers openly questioned whether or not I was a real minister. Some thought Real Live Preacher might be a spoof or a hoax of some kind. Others wondered if perhaps I was trying to convert people and infiltrate the Salon blog community with a hidden Christian agenda. The truth is, I had no desire to convince anyone of anything. I wanted only to write about the things that were important to me, which is what all bloggers do.

Within a week or two I noticed that twenty-five to fifty people were dropping by each day to read what I had written. Many of them left encouraging or challenging comments. I began getting to know other bloggers. I was thrilled and energized. This was fun.

And then one day I logged onto the Salon community server and found that six hundred people had visited Real Live Preacher that very day. I was terrified for some reason and had to leave the room. Real Live Preacher was becoming somewhat well-known in the virtual world of bloggers that is sometimes referred to as "The Blogosphere." E-mails started pouring in. Some people wanted to tell me that my writing had been meaningful to them. Others wanted to ask theological questions. A few wanted advice. And there were angry e-mails. Some of my essays contain "colorful" words. Quite a few people were upset that a minister would use such language.

Christopher Key, a fellow Salon blogger, suggested that I had started a new kind of online ministry. I rejected this outright and with some irritation. I didn't want another ministry. I didn't want to feel responsible for how people responded to my writing. This was MY weblog. I started it for selfish reasons, and I wanted to be selfish about it. People could come and read if they wanted, but I didn't want anyone to suggest that this was a ministry. Ministry meant responsibility, and I didn't want any more of that.

My passionate overreaction to Christopher's observation was probably a sign that, in my heart, I knew he was correct. If I had been honest, I would have admitted that I had already begun to care deeply about how people were reacting to my writing. How could I not care? What made me think I would ever be able to write with no connection to the readers? Even if such a thing is possible, it probably isn't possible for me.

Real Live Preacher was indeed becoming a kind of virtual community, whether I liked it or not. People posted scores of comments at the bottom of my essays, sometimes as many as seventy-five or even a hundred. Real Live Preacher's comments became a chat room of sorts. People began to respond to each other's comments, sometimes without much regard to the subject of the essay. Conversations sprang up and friendships were formed. Atheists, agnostics, Christians, pagans, and people of every imaginable worldview were exchanging ideas pleasantly and, apart from a few exceptions, without becoming angry or defensive. A number of frequent Real Live Preacher commenters were even inspired to launch their own weblogs.

I decided there was no use worrying about what was happening with Real Live Preacher. I would stick to my original plan as best I could. I would work hard at writing and strive to be honest, trying not to worry too much about how my writing was being received and what effect it was or was not having on people. If what I wrote prompted someone to send me an e-mail, I felt compelled to respond politely and with compassion.

Somewhere along the way, a few people from my church discovered Real Live Preacher. It didn't take them long to figure out that the man behind the weblog was their own pastor. Word began to get out, so I went ahead and told the leaders of our church about it. Those in my congregation who know about my blog have been gracious, understanding, and even affirming. Even so, I now have filters that I didn't have before. I write with the knowledge that people in my church will be reading. That's okay. Honest writing always takes place within a given context. My context has just changed a little. I pray that my commitment to honesty has not.

As surprising as the growing popularity of Real Live Preacher was, nothing could have prepared me for the day I opened an email from Chuck Van Hof, a senior editor at Eerdmans. Chuck's email was short and to the point. "Dear Preacher, I would like to talk to you about the book you really need to publish."

I thought it was my friend Larry playing a joke on me. But no, Chuck was exactly who he said he was. That email opened a new chapter in my life. I began to see myself as a serious writer, and I gave myself permission to work harder at my craft. Chuck and I agreed that a collection of Real Live Preacher's essays might make a nice book.

I struggled with the question of whether or not I should remain anonymous, authoring the book under the pseudonym "Real Live Preacher." I even posed the question to the readers of my weblog, and there was some lively debate on the subject. In the end I decided to let the mysterious Real Live Preacher come out of the closet. Maintaining anonymity takes a lot of work, and I had grown tired of it.

So, for all of you who wondered about the man who always signed his e-mail as rlp . . .

Here I am.

I want to thank Scott Rosenberg and Salon.com for providing server space for the Salon weblog community. I am grateful to all the Salon bloggers for making me feel at home and for showing me kindness, patience, and understanding. In my spiritual tradition these things are known as gifts of the Spirit.

To my blogging friends I say, Keep writing and being honest. You are changing the world slowly and from the inside out.

I am especially thankful to Chuck Van Hof for seeing something in me that I did not see in myself. And I want to thank the people of Covenant Baptist Church in San Antonio for letting me be more than just their minister. I have found true friendship in this community. You love me in spite of and because of everything.

Thank you, Mom and Dad, for the border, the books, the bedtime, and the boundaries. Thank you, Janan and Hugh, for walking with me in the misty memory days of childhood.

I dedicate this book to the three sisters, who surround me like a heavenly constellation. And to Jeanene, who is my dearest friend and my wife. We know in our shared heart that we can count on each other to be there until forever comes.

Deep sea Preacher

There is a deep vent on the ocean floor of humanity, a place of creation between belief and unbelief. On this living ridge is the sacred spot where faith takes its first deep breath. This is the womb of grace.

People pop out of this fissure. Young and old, they swirl for a time in a warm eddy before settling on one side or the other.

For better or for worse, I have thrown my Texas lasso into this vent, and now I float above the rift, hanging tight to my rope, fighting the currents.

Peter Pan? Burr under the saddle? Bodhisattva to the agnostic? I don't know what I am. I did not know what I was doing when I cast my rope.

Some of the people drift so naturally into belief, and I shout "Vaya con Dios" while they disappear to one side of the ridge. Others are swept just as naturally to the other side. They take life straight, like Hemingway said.

To them I say, "Be strong. Keep your heart open, as well as your eyes. Keep asking."

"We will, Preacher," they say, their voices growing faint as they follow their current.

"Why are you here?" someone asked as she drifted away. All I gave her was a shrug and a smile because I don't know myself.

I look at my rope-burned hands, and I have no answer.

I only know that I never get tired of living in the moment when faith is born into this world.

The Preacher

A question for the Preacher

"Preacher, how do you know you've chosen the right path? Have you read the Upanishads, the Koran, the Vedas, the Talmud, and others? Have you checked into other religions and compared them with Christianity?"

I'm flattered, but you vastly overestimate the Preacher's intellect, stamina, and attention span. Where are you in your threescore and ten, I wonder? I'm in my forties and have miles to go before deep sleep. I will not have time to explore even the depths of Christianity, though I'm digging as fast as I can.

I can look up from my trench and give a respectful nod to the Buddhist, but I cannot join her and I suspect she cannot join me. It's a matter of time, specifically the lack of it.

Because of my history and where I live, Christianity is my choice. I'm not qualified to make comparisons, but I will claim that my tradition has deep roots and serious bona fides.

In this life you MUST choose. You may limit yourself to handling and re-handling observable data. You may dabble in several faith traditions, but your trenches will be shallow. Or you may choose a spiritual path and love God, as you understand her, with your heart, soul, mind, and strength, working your way ever deeper and ever closer to the reality that you long for.

The Preacher

A preacher, a rabbi, and a professor go into a computer store

I met Rabbi Jonah in a computer store. He was like Santa Claus in a wheelchair. Very fat with a white beard and two thin stockings called legs hung with care from under his great bottom. Polio. He lived back in those days.

His friend Robert had muscular dystrophy and sat quietly in his own wheelchair. Robert had a Ph.D. in history, but his teaching days were over. His new challenge was getting food to his mouth since his arms had begun to fail him.

Thus began a most wonderful and challenging friendship.

Jonah was the most intelligent man I'd ever met. He had a hell of an education too — Old School. He was fluent in at least six languages. He taught himself Greek just so he could look into this "New" Testament.

We quickly settled into the routine that we enjoyed until they moved to Los Angeles two years later. I would load them into their van and drive them all over town. The only agenda was that we never stopped talking. God, religion, history, life, all of it.

That December I was using the Hebrew word Shalom in my Advent sermon series. The rabbi was waxing eloquent on the concept of Shalom while we drank coffee at their kitchen table. I was a little distracted watching Robert trying to steer spoons of soup into his mouth.

I think Jonah realized that he was not at peace and decided to do something about it. He stopped his lesson and asked me point blank, "Do you think I'm going to hell?"

I gave my polite answer. "That's really not my business. What happens to you after you die is between you and God."

That was not enough for the rabbi, who responded quickly. "No, you don't get off that easy. As I understand it, your religious tradition teaches that I will go to hell unless I accept Jesus as my savior. I don't intend to do that. I think you owe me an answer. Do you believe I'm going to hell?"

I did not want to hear this.

He was right. I do come from a tradition that understands hell to be real. Maybe not eternal fire, pitchforks, and gloomy caves, but separation from God is understood to be real.

I'd been avoiding the subject of hell for some time, living in denial. We gentle Christians often do this. The harsh reality of our theology works against what we discover in real life. Those of us who get to know people of other faiths are profoundly moved by the experience.

A Real Live Rabbi faced me across the table. Here was no theology or doctrine or tradition. Here sat Jonah, a man I had grown to love.

He escaped the concentration camps when he was three because a Mennonite man grabbed him and said, "This is my son." His family stared straight ahead and pretended not to know him. They found their pitch basket at the last minute and put him into the river. The Mennonite brought him to this country and helped him find his only surviving relative.

As a young man in rabbinical training he danced with the Torah before polio took his legs.

I went to the synagogue with him and saw him twitching in his chair, for he longed to dance again with the sacred scroll. I heard his impassioned prayers, offered at the end of the day. He was teaching me a little Hebrew, ever patient as I struggled with the text.

I found it hard to look him in the eyes for I understood then how our theology hurt him and other people of faith.

"No," I said. "I do NOT believe you are going to hell. You love God more than anyone I know. More than anyone. I feel closer to you than I do to many in my own tradition. I cannot believe that about you."

He stared at me until I could look him in the eyes again and simply said, "Thank you."

The stunning dignity he put into that "thank you" is ever on my mind.

We have a belief that tells us faith in Jesus Christ is important. We have a theology that tells us what we decide here on earth has consequences after our life is over.

I have two friends named Jonah and Robert. They are Jews. I am unable to think that God does not accept them — I am not able to think this. There is something deep within me that will not abide such thought.

I owe Jonah a great debt. Because of my encounter with him, mine is a theology born not only of word, but of flesh and Spirit.

The Preacher

Tamales

I live in South Texas, where tamales are an important part of life. We know from tamales.

The difference between a good tamal and a bad one is like the difference between a hot, Krispy Kreme delicacy and that half doughnut you found on the floor of your car.

The first time I had real tamales, I ate eight of them in ten minutes. I only stopped because it was getting ridiculous.

It's the masa, or dough, that makes or breaks a tamal. Good ones are moist and savory. They melt in your mouth and make you groan with desire.

Christmas is the traditional time to be making tamales and the time of year that Hispanic women pass on the secrets of this ancient art to their daughters and granddaughters. The best tamales come from their kitchens, but you have to be a friend of the family to get some.

The Preacher's tips for eating tamales:

1. Do not eat the corn shuck wrapper, Yankee.

2. Do not put salsa or chili on a tamal, not on a good one anyway. That's . . . unseemly.

3. A fresh jalapeno is a nice complement. Fresh, not those pickled abominations. Slice it up and take your chances. Fresh peppers vary greatly in how much heat they pack. If the pepper is hot, one slice will light you up for the duration. You learn to manage your peppers to keep a nice burn going. Nice, but not too much.

People who love hot peppers surf the line between pain and pleasure for the endorphin rush.

4. Have plenty of cold beer and flour tortillas on hand for first aid.

In most South Texas towns you can find a restaurant that makes tamales in the traditional way, with lots of love and no shortcuts, but you will have to be on a serious quest.

Reynaldo's is that restaurant in our town. It took me five years to find it.

You don't go into Reynaldo's to buy tamales. You knock at the side door of the kitchen and speak with Lupe. There are three large stoves, each with six huge, steaming pots on top. You buy tamales by the dozen. Lupe scoops them out and wraps them in butcher paper and foil.

If you are smart you will ask for one and eat it right on the spot. At first you will not be able to speak. When you can speak, your words will be given by the Holy Spirit.

"Oh my God" seems to be the most common utterance among Anglos. "Madre de Dios," among Hispanics.

Lupe has been making tamales at Reynaldo's for forty years.

While I was in high school, she was making tamales.

While I went to college, she was making tamales.

While I struggled with God in seminary, she was making tamales.

While you and I pour out our souls and struggle with issues of faith and life, she is making tamales.

She makes and serves tamales. That is her life.

Do you think her life is less fulfilling than yours or mine, less interesting and less actualized?

You wouldn't think so if you ate her tamales with your closest friends. If you let the jalapeno arouse and the masa soothe you, if you felt the endorphins release into the buzz from your beer and felt your passion for your friends rise until you could not contain your laughter, then you would not think so. You would praise the name of Lupe and marvel at what she gives this world.

There would not be tamales if there were not people like Lupe.

The women who make tamales in our town are some of the most Christ-like people I know. They give their lives away so that something good may come into this world.

The Preacher

The Preacher's story

Part 1: I am a strange mix

The preacher grew up in a devout Baptist family in Texas. Some of you
are imagining a domineering father and endless hours of religious abuse
punctuated with occasional beatings.

Not so.

I have a great family. My parents were and are gentle Christians who
put a premium on living a Christ-like life and helping the poor. We lived
in the border town of El Paso, and my mother and father were actively
involved with a group of Christians who were constantly throwing their
resources at the piteous poverty that coexisted with us just on the other
side of the Rio Grande.

I spent a lot of time in Mexico as a young boy. The Preacher knows
the mingled smells of outhouses, kerosene, and poverty. It's something
you never forget.

One year during a bitter cold spell my father and his friends showed
up at the border with a load of blankets and coats. The forecast was for
temperatures well below freezing that night, and they knew a lot of fami-
lies were going to be cold. The Mexican government forbade them from
entering. Some bureaucratic bullshit, I guess.

My dad said his kinder, gentler equivalent of "screw it" and became a
smuggler on the spot. He and the others made numerous trips across the
border that day in their cars with blankets, food, and jackets crammed
under the seats and hidden in the trunks.

My dad felt that one's calling to serve God was higher than one's calling to obey the law. For Christ's sake, he and his friends couldn't let children freeze.

"For Christ's sake" packs a punch when you mean it literally.

My family went to services three and four times a week. Ours was a nice church filled with good people who cherished one another. I enjoyed being a part of the community and learned to love Jesus in that place.

These were the Christian people who nurtured me and taught me my faith.

I came to understand that it was the teachings of that same Jesus that led my parents to fight poverty and want in the border town.

There was a leeetle problem though. Early on it became apparent that something was different about me. I couldn't make myself believe some parts of the Bible. I was a natural born skeptic.

When told the "Noah and the Ark" story in Sunday School, I quickly figured out that two of every kind of animal would not fit on one boat. No one else seemed to be doing the math. I could no more believe the ark story than I could believe the sky was green. I wanted to believe. Believing seemed nice, but I couldn't. I COULD NOT.

I felt strange and out of place because everyone else at church seemed to believe everything.

I kept my "believing problem" to myself because I thought something was wrong with me.

Thus was born the strange dichotomy that has become the Preacher. A passionate love for Christ and his teachings mingled with a fierce skepticism that would only grow stronger as I grew older.

Part 2: College, seminary, and disillusionment

I felt "the call" to ministry after high school. Let's just say I had a strong desire to be of service to God, and I wanted to learn more about the now troublesome Bible.

I went to a university and majored in religious studies with minors in Greek and philosophy. Except for the philosophy, that's a standard "pre-seminary" degree. Eye opening time! I discovered most serious Bible scholars had moved beyond a simplistic reading of scripture.

The bottom line: not everything in the Bible should be taken literally, and, more importantly, not everything in the Bible applies to MY life.

After college I spent four years in seminary studying further. I managed to work out my problems with scripture and now believe the Bible won't cause insurmountable problems for anyone willing to study it with integrity.

I was, however, experiencing disillusionment of another kind. The source of this new trouble was my growing dissatisfaction with a lot of the Christian people I was meeting.

Sometimes it seemed Christian people literally took leave of their senses. Once I was at a gathering with Christians who were singing some kind of spiritual song. One of the lines included the hideous phrase, *"I've never seen God's children begging for bread."*

I was sickened. "What about those kids I saw in Mexico?" Were they suggesting those hungry kids were not God's children? I decided these people were living in a dream world. All they wanted to do was sing songs about Jesus and pretend the world was wonderful. The world IS wonderful, but it also contains great evil and sadness.

It seemed to me that many Christians saw only what they wanted to see. They needed the world to fit easily into their categories.

Over the eight years of my formal theological education, I encountered many such examples of Christians who, I felt, were not living honest and authentic lives.

By the time I was out of school and ready to be an employed minister, I was having some serious problems with the church. That's not good. My options were pretty much "minister" or "you want fries with that?"

One

I believed then and still believe that many Christians are not honest about their own failings, sins, and disappointments. Like Martha Stewart, they try to sell a sugary, imaginary world of happiness to people who are hurting and looking for real answers.

Two

I believed then and still believe that many Christians use manipulative techniques to win converts. The pursuit of truth has taken a back seat or has been lost altogether. What matters is numbers, namely how many people you can convince to become Christians. Converts are counted and boasted about. They wouldn't call it boasting, but that's what it is. Retch!

Three

I believed then and still believe that many Christians have created a subculture with its own language, customs, and myths. Ministers even have their own dialect and hairdos. Weird. This subculture is really more about worshipping America than God, more about achieving than receiving, more about competition than grace. The problem with a religious subculture is no one else "gets it," and you are isolated from the world you are called to SERVE.

Four

I became increasingly disgusted with the institutional and bureaucratic nature of churches. It seemed to me that many churches were worshipping the idols of wealth, power, and prestige. It seemed to me that many churches existed solely to support the Christian subculture.

I could write for an hour about each of these, but the Preacher counts brevity as a virtue.

In spite of these troubles, I still believed that something beautiful was possible for the Church. I dreamed of finding a small community of people, dedicated to Christ and to bringing God's love to the world. These people would be bold enough to live authentic lives and not be tied to a Christian subculture.

I would say I longed for a spiritual journey and not a religious assimilation.

Part 3: Dark night of the soul

After seminary I started a chaplain internship. The program was called "Clinical Pastoral Education," sometimes referred to as "Tear the Young Minister a New One."

I trundled my idealistic, educated self to the hospital. I was fresh out of seminary and used to sitting around talking about higher criticism.

This hospital gig was just the kick in the ass I needed.

You see, people facing death don't give a damn about your interpretation of 2 Timothy. Some take the "bloodied, but unbowed" road, but most dying people want to pray with the chaplain. And they don't want wimpy prayers either. They don't want you to pray that God's will be done.

Hell no. People want you to get down and dirty with them. They want to call down angels and the powers of the Almighty. THEY ARE DYING and the whole world should stop.

I threw myself into it. I prayed holding hands and cradling heads. I prayed with children and old men. I prayed with a man who lost his tongue to cancer. I lent him mine. I prayed my ass off. I had fifty variations of every prayer you could imagine, one hell of a repertoire.

I started noticing something. When the doctors said someone was going to die, they did. When they said 10 percent chance of survival, about nine out of ten died. The odds ran pretty much as predicted by the physicians. I mean, was this praying doing ANYTHING?

I'm sophisticated enough to understand the value of human contact, but prayer is supposed to affect the outcome, right?

I began to feel the "ping" of a tiny hammer, tapping away at my faith.

Then I met Jenny.

Thirty something. Cute. New mother with two little kids. Breast cancer. Found it too late. Spread all over. Absolutely going to die.

Jenny had only one request. "I know I'm going to die, chaplain. I need time to finish this. It's for my kids. Pray with me that God will give me the strength to finish it."

She showed me the needlepoint pillow she was making for her children. It was an "alphabet blocks and apples" kind of thing. She knew she would not be there for them. Would not drop them off at kindergarten, would not see baseball games, would not help her daughter pick out her first bra. No weddings, no grandkids. Nothing.

She had this fantasy that her children would cherish this thing — sleep with it, snuggle it. Someday it might be lovingly put on display at her daughter's wedding. Perhaps there would be a moment of silence. Some part of her would be there.

I was totally hooked. We prayed. We believed. Jesus, this was the kind of prayer you *could* believe in. We were like idiots and fools.

A couple of days later I went to see her only to find the room filled with doctors and nurses. She was having violent convulsions and terrible pain. I watched while she died hard. Real hard.

As the door shut, the last thing I saw was the unfinished needlepoint lying on the floor.

Ping. The hammer fell and preacher came tumbling after.

It's funny, when your faith finally caves, it goes all at once. You realize you were just a shell held together with hackneyed rituals and desperate hopes. You are not strong. You do not have answers.

I don't remember the walk back to the office. I must have had the classic, "Young chaplain just got the shit kicked out of him" look because people left me alone.

I looked in the restroom mirror and said, "I do not believe in God." I knew this was the truth and felt the need to say it out loud. I was on the other side now. I was an unbeliever. It was like waking up in Tokyo and noticing to your great surprise that you've become Japanese. You weren't raised in Japan, and you have no idea how to use chopsticks. What the hell are you gonna do with yourself?

It wasn't the experience with Jenny that caused my break with God. It was the kids in Mexico, my difficulty in believing parts of the Bible, the phony Christians I met along the way, and the hundreds of prayers that seemed unanswered. Jenny was just the last blow from a hammer that had been working on my foundation for a long time.

St. John of the Cross calls it "The Dark Night of the Soul." He says those seeking God will walk the paths of others but eventually those paths will end and there will be no path. They will be left with "Nada, Nada, Nada." Nothing, Nothing, Nothing.

It broke my heart. I grieved in joint and marrow. My reptilian brain cried. I was sad all the way to the bottom.

Part 4: The Preacher is out of his tiny mind

I received an e-mail from someone puzzled about the grief I experienced when I gave up on God. This person felt liberated when she left Christianity.

I understand how some would feel that way. Many of you only know Christianity from bad books, TV preachers, and the people who watch them. If that were all I knew of Christianity I would celebrate my liberation from it all the days of my life.

But I was exposed early to the real stuff — Top Shelf Christianity — Deep and Old Christianity. This kind is practiced by people who work until they stink and take life in great draughts. Their hands are as rough as their hides, and they DO their faith in secret, hiding their good works in obedience to Christ. They know how to love and be loved in return. Their laughter is loud and has its roots in joy.

These Christians don't want your money and they don't advertise. You will only find them if you MUST find them. These are the ones who took me to Mexico as a boy and showed me pain and joy. They hid nothing from me.

I was also blessed by being exposed to the right kind of Christian thinkers. C. S. Lewis and his friend J. R. R. Tolkien. Frederick Buechner, Carlyle Marney, and Thomas Merton. Will Campbell who wrote *Brother to a Dragonfly* and Eberhard Arnold. Frederick Dale Bruner and Martin Luther King, Jr.

You did understand there was more to Christianity than religious TV and the drivel they sell in those awful Christian bookstores, right? After all, Christianity didn't sustain itself for twenty centuries by shitting Hallmark cards before a live studio audience.

Hell yes, I grieved. I thought not "believing" in God meant losing this life and, worse, losing these people.

I decided not to give up without a fight. I *can* be a *stubborn* son-of-a-bitch. I sought answers. I read the good stuff and talked with the good people.

I learned some things. I found my way.

Turns out Christianity is an Eastern religion. The earliest Christians were Hebrews. Semites. People of the East. They did not know how to separate mind from body. They were holistic before holistic was cool.

In our world we *have* separated mind from body to our great loss. Here a man may betray his wife and neglect his children, but say he loves them "down inside."

Bullshit. There is no "down inside." Love is something you do, not something you feel.

Likewise, we think having faith means being convinced God exists in the same way we are convinced a chair exists. People who cannot be completely convinced of God's existence think faith is impossible for them.

Not so. People who doubt can have great faith because *faith is something you do, not something you think*. In fact, the greater your doubt the more heroic your faith.

I learned that it doesn't matter in the least that I be convinced of God's existence. Whether or not God exists is none of my business, really. What do I know of existence? I don't even know how the VCR works.

What *does* matter is whether or not I am faithful. I think "faithful" is a hell of a good word. It still has some of its original shine. It still calls us to action.

Once I stumbled upon this very old truth, I prayed the most honest prayer of my life.

God, I don't have great faith, but I can be faithful. My belief in you may be seasonal, but my faithfulness will not. I will follow in the way of Christ. I will act as though my life and the lives of others matter. I will love.

I have no greater gift to offer than my life. Take it.

That's it. I pushed all my chips across the table. The Preacher bet it all. Why? Because the idea that there is a God who cares for us busts my heart wide open. Because I pushed reason as far as it can go but I wanted to go farther still. Because I wanted to, and . . . well . . . I just wanted to.

I'm an idiot and out of my mind, and I don't care who knows it. Sue me.

"And what does the Lord require of you, O man, but to do justice, love kindness, and walk humbly with God." Micah 6:8

Postscript

I've been working this simple spiritual program for sixteen years now. I seek to be faithful to what my tradition teaches me about God. I fall short much of the time. I ask forgiveness and move on.

After sixteen years God gave me two gifts.

Prayer became a joy again. I sit in silence more than I speak nowadays. I've been known to sneak into churches on weekdays and take naps in the pews. I know it sounds crazy, but it feels like God is watching me when I nap in church, and I like that.

Sometimes I "feel" that God exists. After all this time, that's nice, but not necessary anymore.

My old demons still haunt me. Voices whisper to me on dark nights, saying, "You know there is no God. You're wasting your life and you are a fool."

I hear the voices, but they have very little power over me because you know I'm not going to stop now.

The Preacher

Why don't you write something about prayer?

"Why don't you write something about prayer?"

"About prayer? Whaddya mean?"

"Just about prayer is all. I don't know, it seems like that's a part that's missing. You write about everything else. You do pray, right?"

"Well yeah, but . . ."

"So okay, why don't you write something about it? I think that would be nice if you wrote something about prayer."

"Yeah? I don't know."

"See, that's what I don't get about you. Sometimes I think you're this deep person. You know, spiritual. And then sometimes you're like . . . something."

"I'm like, SOMETHING?"

"I couldn't think of a comparison. You're like a preacher who won't write about prayer, I guess. I don't understand that."

"OKAY, I'll write about prayer."

"Good."

"I'll just write something."

"That's all I'm sayin."

"I DO pray, you know? It's not like I don't."

"Okay."

"Only if I do this, I'd want people to understand that you can't tell anyone how to pray. That's what I hate about a lot of things that are written about prayer. They sound like instruction manuals. It's not origami."

"Yours wouldn't be like that. You'd write it good."

"Maybe . . . I don't know. Anyway, I'd also want people to understand something else. You don't pray so you can change things in the world. It's not magic.

You might ask, and you might hope for change, but ultimately changing things cannot be your motivation. That's important."

"Yeah, I guess. Sure."

"I'll tell you something else. It's going to be hard to get all that into an essay and still have room to say anything about praying. I mean, by the time you set those conditions and explain all that, you're done. You've used up all your energy. You've gone in that direction, and it would be hard as hell to bend the essay around to where you could say anything positive about prayer. Hard as hell."

"I'm sure you'll think of something."

Something about prayer

What's the weirdest thing I ever prayed for in church?

A hermit crab.

A little girl raised her hand and asked if the whole congregation would pray for her sick hermit crab. I don't remember exactly what was wrong with this crab. I don't know how you determine that a hermit crab is ailing in the first place. She seemed pretty sure he was sick, so we took her word for it.

Among those who bowed their heads that day was Roy, whose father died when he was nine. This was back in the Great Depression. His mother was left alone to scratch out an existence for herself and her two small boys there in the flatlands of the Texas Panhandle.

Chris was there that morning, too. Her father abused her for years and years, and no one in her family ever came to her rescue. As I recall, she used to sit in church when she was a little girl and pray that he would stop. I sneaked a glance at Chris and saw her head go down.

There were others with similar stories. The room was full of people who had been through hard times and done plenty of praying along the way.

It's funny how a preacher's mind can wander, right in the middle of a sermon or even just before a prayer. I couldn't help but think of Julie, the little girl I prayed for years ago. She was five years old and had vaginal cancer. I prayed first that she would be healed and later that she would die in peace. The silence leading up to her very painful death was deafening. When it was over I said to God, "I'll take that as a 'no.'"

All the heads bowed except mine. I was left standing at the front, wondering how you pray for a hermit crab in the presence of a man who prayed that his daddy would live. How do you pray for a hermit crab while looking at the bowed head of a woman who prayed that her daddy would stop?

And what about Julie, God? Exactly what was going on with that situation? Maybe it's like the butterfly that causes a hurricane on the other side of the planet. Maybe you have complex reasons for taking a hands-off approach. But what grand scheme would have been derailed if you had let her die without pain?

If letting Julie die in peace was outside your self-imposed limits, what will you do for a hermit crab that we hear is a little under the weather?

Like I said, it's funny how a preacher's mind can wander. The people in my church have gotten used to the occasional pause before I begin to pray. This was one of the longer ones.

You know what got me started praying? The heads. Roy's head and Chris's head. All of them. Rows and rows of bowed heads, waiting expectantly. Toward the back I saw the head of the little girl who asked for this prayer. Her hands were clasped in front of her so seriously. It was a precious sight, and my heart was filled with love for these people. I was like the Grinch looking down on the little town of Who-ville and having a stunning revelation of his own.

"Maybe prayer," I thought, "means a little bit more."

Here were people who would pray for a crab. They loved this little girl that much, and she felt comfortable enough to share the concerns of her heart. Even in the midst of their own unanswered prayers, they were big enough and small enough to pray with their young friend.

And then I wanted to be like these people. I wanted to be praying with them, and I didn't care if it made sense or not. I said to myself, "The hell with it. I'm praying for the damn crab."

And I did.

When the prayer was over, all the heads came up and no one knew what had happened to me. As far as they knew, a kid had asked for prayer and we had prayed. Business as usual.

But it wasn't business as usual for me. Whatever I was praying for, I got what I needed. And I did not miss the irony either. The one leading the prayer knew less about praying than almost anyone in the room, including the little girl who loved her hermit crab.

That little girl was my daughter, by the way. The second of three sisters. The crab was named "Pinchy," and he lived in our house all the days of his life.

I am a man who has become a child again, and I tell you I will pray for just about anything.

The Preacher

Forget the angles

I have a preacher friend who lives in an old farmhouse that he is restoring himself. He's one of those "do everything" guys. Gardening, carpentry, repair work, he does it all.

Robert is no bullshit, pantywaist, white-collar preacher with soft theology and a degree in marketing. His faith and knowledge are deep and wide. He started his real learning after seminary.

The best thing I can say about him is this: his heart is soft enough to be broken, and his hands are strong enough to mend your shed.

A few months ago Robert hosted a retreat at his farm for misfit pastors. There were four of us, all slightly irregular, all in danger of not passing inspection. Hell, a couple of us have already been rejected and are now on the discount table.

I was wandering through the rooms, admiring the old farmhouse, when Robert said, "You know what I love most about this place?"

"What?"

"You won't find a 90-degree angle anywhere."

I ran my hand up and down the nearest corner and looked at it closely. He was right. The angle was acute by about 10 degrees. The next corner was an obtuse mirror of the first. Euclid says I didn't need to check the other corners, but you know I did. And yes, they were all irregular.

"Robert, how can the angles be this far off? Was the guy who built it a spectacularly bad carpenter, or has it shifted over the years?"

Robert didn't look at me when he replied. He was looking at the wall and running his hand back and forth over it, like you'd run your hand down a horse's flank. "It was built this way, and the man was a wonderful carpenter. He just didn't care about 90-degree angles."

I was confused. How can you be a good carpenter and not care about right angles? I shook my head, not understanding. "Is it safe? Why hasn't it fallen apart? How does it hold together?"

He smiled. "How indeed? And yet, here it stands, apparently doing quite well for itself these last 125 years. There's nothing sacred about 90 degrees. You're worshipping at the wrong altar. What you want are straight walls and good joints. You connect four straight walls, and the angles will take care of themselves. They will always come out to a perfect 360 degrees. Why worry about it? God's got your back!"

I experienced a moment of mental slippage. Ninety-degree angles meant craftsmanship and solidity to me, and I resisted letting this go. I had a vision of a Dr. Seuss house with strange walls jutting out at bizarre angles.

And then the scales fell from my eyes, and I could see. In my mind I saw an imaginary floor plan. The interior walls were not perpendicular to the exterior walls, but all the angles were snuggling. Every acute was spooning with its obtuse mate.

I saw the truth of it, and I loved the truth.

All I could say was "Holy Shit!"

Robert jerked his head toward the kitchen. The coffee was ready, and the other guys were gathering. I followed him, rolling this new thought around in my head and loving the feel of it. Four connected, straight walls will always have angles that total 360 degrees. What have we been worrying about?

"Rob, I don't know if it's God or geometry, but something's definitely watching out for us."

We took our seats with the other misfits, and there we were. Four irregulars joined perfectly around a sacred wooden table. Robert poured himself a cup of coffee and had his last say on the matter.

"God. Geometry. What's the difference? Be straight, and make good connections. Don't feel like you have to know all the angles. Let things work themselves out.

"As for the carpenter who built this house, I think he was a lot like another carpenter I've read about."

The Preacher

The Preacher is tired tonight

Sundays can be a bitch.

I get up way before daylight and head for church. I open up the joint. I putter around and straighten hymnals. I make ready. I preach the sermon three or four times. I talk to myself. I talk to God out loud. I light candles and pray. Sometimes I throw a nerf football around the sanctuary while I get my mind straight. *You should try that sometime if you can find a church that will let you get away with it.*

None of this is what makes Sunday hard.

What's hard about Sunday is that I don't matter on this day. Sunday is for the folks who come to church. It's their day and not mine. I must be "up" when everyone arrives. I must be emotionally ready.

Anyone who has children understands what I'm talking about. If you are a daddy, you always make the left turn and take your paycheck and yourself home to your kids. One day you may feel like turning right and leaving town, but you don't. How you feel on one given day is not really the issue.

I believe love is primarily a choice and only sometimes a feeling. If you want to feel love, choose to love and be patient.

Okay, so when I made a commitment to shepherd these people, I made a conscious decision to love them. That commitment is more important than how I feel come Sunday morning. I *will* be there early. I *will* set things up. I *will* do the early morning candle/praying/nerf thing. I *will* be ready.

I do this every single Sunday. I do this when I am sad. I do this when I am depressed. I do this when I am hurting inside.

I do this many Sundays when I don't believe in God.

On those days I stare at the door to the church in the dark. The silence of the building is reminiscent of the silence of God. I say, "fuck it" and go on in. I do the candle/praying/nerf thing. I make ready. I *will* be glad to see them. I *will* love the children. I *will* stop for a moment and talk to the woman who needs too much. I *will* preach, one more time.

Fidelity to commitment in the face of doubts and fears is a very spiritual thing. I don't suggest it for the weak of heart or if you are in a hurry. An old preacher once said, *"Until you've stood at the door for years and knocked until your knuckles bleed, you don't know what prayer is."*

I'd like to have met that preacher.

I wonder how much longer I'll do this? I have no idea. I live week to week.

On Sunday after church I feel numb all over. I mean that literally. I AM NUMB. I got nothin' left for nobody.

The Preacher lives for Sunday night. Sunday night is when *I* matter. On Sunday night I sing the Song of Myself. I pop in the latest thing from Netflix, drink too much diet coke, and eat more than I should. I settle into the couch and take care of myself.

I do this every Sunday night except I didn't tonight. Tonight I wrote this. And the Preacher feels better. And the Preacher is going to bed.

The Preacher

Flower children

There's a charismatic church meeting in our building on Saturday nights. Perhaps you don't know what charismatic Christians are. Let's see, how can I explain this?

If Baptist Fundamentalists are like cowboys who put their pointy-toed boots up your ass and then smile at you, charismatic Christians are like flower children. It's all lovin' and dancin' with these guys. They spend a big part of their worship service singing songs to Jesus, and they cry a lot. When they pray they hold their hands in the air, palms upward. They dance and sway to their music.

Sometimes they get carried away and speak in tongues. There's something very childlike about this. It's like baby talk. Jesus called God "abba," the Aramaic equivalent of "dada," so I guess it's okay. I don't speak in tongues, myself. I'm way too self-conscious for that sort of thing, and, to be honest, I think it's kind of goofy. But, like my friend Earl the grave digger says, "Whatever gets you through the night."

I like the flower children. They're very nice and they have a warmth about them. Sometimes I sit in the back during their service to watch the action and enjoy the music. They rock, too — electric guitars, tambourines, and congas. Hell, they can speak in tongues all they want as far as I am concerned.

When their service is over, I like to arrange the chairs for ours. It means one less thing for me to do in the morning. The flower children always offer to help, but I don't let them. I think the best part of church is hanging around afterward and chatting with friends. I don't want them to miss that important sacrament.

Also, I'm a bit compulsive about the way I arrange chairs. I don't ask anyone to help so I can feel free to indulge this part of my personality.

I've noticed the flower children are pretty sloppy with their chairs. This makes sense. Everything is just going to get shoved around when the dancing starts anyway.

I said in one of my earlier posts that Sundays can be a bitch. Last Sunday was one of those. I didn't go to the church on Saturday night because I was already getting depressed. I knew I'd have to do the chairs in the morning, but procrastination was my first love, and she still works for me sometimes.

I got up Sunday and felt like shit. I had to drag my sorry-ass all the way to church, and I did not want to be there. Standing at the door to the church on a dark winter morning is no fun when I'm having one of "those Sundays."

I took a deep breath and went inside. I turned on the lights and discovered that the flower children had arranged the chairs just the way I like them.

I've been using my *"three sides of a rectangle with corner aisles at 45 degrees"* arrangement lately. You start with nine chairs on the back rows, then eight, then seven . . . you don't really want to know any more, do you?

I told you I'm weird about the chairs.

They got it exactly right. I promise you, every chair was perfect.

I swear one of them must have watched me for a couple of weeks and taken notes. Imagining the flower children lining up the rows and counting the chairs made me laugh out loud. It was a very nice gesture of love and it couldn't have come at a better time.

Something changed inside me, and I was glad to be in church again.

There's this book called *The Tipping Point*. I didn't read it because it's a book about how fads get started and, well, who cares. But I did find out what the title means. When you eat a piece of pie you always reach a point where the pie tips over. There's nothing special about that last bite except that it brought you to the tipping point.

That's what love can do. Even a little bit of it can tip you over when it comes at just the right time.

The Preacher

The Preacher remembers Earl the grave digger

When I was in seminary I worked as a security guard at a local retirement community. This was light security — no guns and lots of cookies. Those darlings were charmed by the young, idealistic seminarian, giving his life to the ministry. *(moment of silence please)* They responded with cookies. The soon-to-be preacher gained a pound every time he made his rounds.

A few months before graduation a new security guard was hired. Earl looked so much like Lurch from "The Adams Family" that people stopped and stared. I was speechless when I met him. 6′ 9″, gaunt, deep voice. Real scary. Earl had an absolutely flat affect. Never joked. Never smiled. Extremely nice but no fooling around.

The first night we were sitting at our desk in the security office, and I asked Earl what he had done before coming to the retirement home. "Grave digger," he said, in his flat tone. He saw nothing funny in that.

There was this wonderful moment where we were looking at each other across the table. I chewed my tongue to keep from laughing. Of course Earl had been a grave digger. Why had I bothered to ask?

Late night security at a retirement home leaves plenty of time for conversation. Incidents are rare and usually rather tame. Once I was called to Mrs. Reynolds's apartment to fetch a strange child she said was crouching under her night table. I arrived and was escorted to the table in question. Under it was a book. The tiny picture of the author on the back of the book jacket was visible. "See," she said. "There he is. He's the strangest child. Never answers. Just sits there looking at me."

Okay.

I removed the book jacket and told Mrs. Reynolds I would see the child safely home. She gave me cookies. I tell ya, I was a hero in those days.

Most nights Earl and I sat around talking. He had the vocabulary of an Oxford Don, and I was stunned by his security reports. "The estimable Gordon successfully completed his rounds and proffered his assistance with mine."

It's the only time in my life I ever proffered anything. I rather liked it. I *really* liked Earl.

Eventually the conversation turned to God. Earl was a thoroughgoing atheist. Not angry. Not defensive. No need to convince anyone to join him. Very rational. He celebrated my calling to the ministry and was genuinely interested in the classes I was taking.

One night we were sitting at our desk and a bookmarker fell out of whatever the hell Earl was reading. It was a construction paper cross with "Jesus loves you Daddy" written on it in crayon.

I picked it up and looked at him. "Earl?"

It was given to him by his daughter who went to church with her mother. Like lots of little kids, she really, really loved Jesus.

I asked Earl if he minded his daughter going to church.

"Absolutely not," he said. "Whatever gets you through the night." He punctuated this with a thumbs-up. "Plus, she gave it to me because she loves me."

At that time the Preacher was newly married. Later I would discover how your child can pull your heart out of your chest with a little gesture like that.

He cradled the small cross in his large hands. For a moment our heads were bowed across the desk in adoration of this little icon of love.

The seminarian giving his life to the service of that cross and the atheist who understood the love of his child shared a moment of worship.

Dear friends, I celebrate our common ground. I marvel at the impulse of love which is clearly present in all of us.

Now I lay me down my need to save or evangelize you. That's not an easy move for a preacher. We've been taught that all souls are our responsibility. That's a terrible burden to bear, and it feels good to let it go.

Thank you for making me welcome. Thank you for letting me tell my stories. I didn't realize how desperately I needed to share them.

The Preacher

How to find a church

I keep getting emails from people who say, "Your church sounds nice. I wish I could find one like that."

Let me guess. You're looking for a cool church, filled with authentic Christians who aren't judgmental, but also have convictions, and are hip and classic in just the right mixture. A church where people forgive each other, and love children, and worship in meaningful ways. A church with a swingin' preacher who makes the Bible come alive, and tells great stories, and is a wonderful inspiration, and plays disk golf too. A church that isn't liberal or conservative, but seems to transcend worthless categories like those. A church where the hunger for truth is honored, and people can disagree but still love each other and share a plate of tacos. A church where people are committed to "The Christ Life" and it shows in the fabulous and creative ways they love the world.

That what you're looking for? I got ya. I understand.

Here are some tips to help you in your search.

1. You won't find that church.

2. Open the yellow pages. Tear out the entire church section and burn it. Offer prayers for your journey while warming yourself at the fire. Dance if that's your thing.

3. Surely I don't need to say anything about churches that have billboards and commercials featuring preachers with $200 haircuts who look at you like the cat who shat in your hat.

4. Dedicate yourself to this quest. Be at least as committed as I was to finding good tamales.

5. Call denominational offices in your town and ask if they know of any spectacularly unsuccessful churches. Explain that you do NOT want

a church that is huge and famous and full of all the right kind of people. Tell them you are looking for a ragged bunch of pilgrims who might be meeting in a Laundromat or someplace like that.

6. Try the Quakers. You'll have a hell of a time finding them, but that's the point.

7. Find out if there are any "house churches" in your area. Not every house church is what you're looking for, but your odds are better. These are Christians who have decided not to have buildings. They put a high premium on authenticity and relationships. Think guitars, Ritz crackers, and singing Jesus songs with a baby in your lap.

8. Let's talk about #1 again. As I said, you won't find the church you're looking for. Go ahead and grieve. You'll have to make do with a silly bunch of dreamers and children, prone to mistakes, blunders, and misjudgments.

Find some people you can hang with — people you can trust. Be patient. You'll change them and they'll change you. You'll meet somewhere in the middle.

Relax. It's all good. God might use this journey to teach you something. If you don't find what you're looking for, you might pick up some friends along the way and start your own church. All you need is coffee, a Bible, and a couple of kindred spirits.

Don't skimp on the coffee. Get the good stuff.

That's what we did — fourteen years ago.

The Preacher

Crocodile hunter

When I first came to know Jonah and Robert, I was very eager to please. They were my first real wheelchair friends. When I was with them my personality took on a quality not unlike that of the Crocodile Hunter on TV. Every request was met with a boisterous "Absolutely."

I hovered over them with manic energy. I was Johnny-on-the-spot. I was here, there, everywhere, pushing in chairs and getting extra napkins. I wasn't so much their friend as their manservant.

I think people in wheelchairs learn to live through this phase with new friends. What happens is you get so tired of being a servant that you either drop the relationship or start treating them like real people.

One day when I was visiting, their paid assistant left to take a few hours off.

Robert dropped a bombshell.

"Gordon, I need you to help me go to the bathroom."

My bold, Crocodile Hunter "Absolutely" withered into "mkay" with the end of the word lilted up like a desperate question.

Robert's hands are permanently clenched in palsied fists. You can jam a spoon in his hand so he can bravely push food toward his mouth, but he has no fine motor skills.

My mind was racing as I considered just what "help me go to the bath-room" might entail. Robert, however, was very calm and absolutely not em-barrassed. "Don't worry," he said. "I'll tell you exactly what you need to do."

I wheeled him into their bathroom, and he walked me through the pro-cess. I followed every step with nervous obedience, like I do when I cook.

"Okay, put your arms under my armpits like you're giving me a hug, and help me stand up."

He held his arms up and I slid mine under his. We were cheek to cheek. He was heavy, but I got him standing.

"Good. Now pull my pants down. They've got to be down near my ankles."

It was hard to pull Robert's pants down — hard to even get started. This was his belt, and his zipper, and his soft belly I was touching.

I knelt in front of him and undid everything. I worked his corduroys and underpants down close to his ankles. He was naked and not ashamed. I was back in The Garden with him and surprised to find that I was not ashamed either.

"Now put your arms around me again, just as before, and help me sit on the toilet." We slow danced with little baby steps until I got him in front of the toilet, then I sat him down.

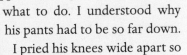

At this point I stopped needing instructions. I saw what to do. I understood why his pants had to be so far down. I pried his knees wide apart so he could use his club of a hand to tuck his genitals between his thighs, and then my work was done.

I walked out p r o f o u n d l y moved. This kind of intimacy was something out of my experience. It was on beyond zebra and outward into the high country. I'd never walked this road before.

I thought I was through, but there was more. Soon I heard Robert calling me from the bathroom. "Gordon, I need you to help me clean up."

Of course he did. How could I not anticipate this? Denial? I don't know, but I froze when I heard him. I had small children at the time, and wiping bottoms was something I did every day. This was different. This was wiping a full-grown man's ass, which disgusted me, and that made me ashamed.

Robert was matter-of-fact and quite dignified. "Okay, lean me forward until my head is almost to my knees. Then you'll be able to clean me."

I pushed him forward and then I saw that the assistant had not been doing a good job of cleaning Robert. He was a mess and not just from *this* bowel movement.

And just like that he became my child.

Occasionally parents come home to find the baby sitter has not been as thorough as she might have been when changing a diaper. It's not hot anger you feel, but you are put out. Little children need you to do a good job cleaning them. Not to do so is to be unkind to the helpless.

At that time my wife and I kept a box of diaper wipes in the car at all times. I sat Robert back up and said, "Hang on a moment. I've got something you're going to like." I ran to my car and got a handful of wipes, which had been nicely warmed by the sun.

I cleaned him and did it right. It wasn't disgusting at all. It was just like cleaning my own children.

When I pushed him back to a sitting position, he said, "Ah, that's nice."

I was never their manservant after that, never the Crocodile hunter again. When someone allows you to bear his burdens, you have found deep friendship.

Such friendships are rare because most of us will fight tooth and nail to bear our own burdens all of our days. We do not want to be dependent on anyone else. We understand that in our dotage someone may have to clean our bottoms, but we look to that day with fear and loathing.

For Robert and Jonah, bearing such burdens is an everyday part of friendship.

There is wisdom here, but it is the kind that cannot be given. It can only happen to you. Watch for it and wait.

The Preacher

Be Thou my vision

I am shy about what I will now write because I know it will make no sense to some of you. I feel like I'm in The Garden with nothing to cover my nakedness.

I've shared my deepest doubts and some high and low moments with you. Now I want to tell you how faith drags itself across the strings of my heart. The vibration comes from far down and long ago.

I was alone at the church this week, setting up chairs and tables for our Wednesday evening meal. There is no formal prayer time on Wednesdays. Our fellowship is our prayer and the Spirit we sense in each other is the answer to that prayer. It is enough and sometimes too much.

As I worked, I was listening to "Celtic Reflections on Hymns," by Eden's Bridge. Their rendition of "Be Thou My Vision" is my favorite song on this CD.

Be Thou my vision, O Lord of my heart,
Be all else but naught to me, save that Thou art;
Be Thou my best thought in the day and the night,
Both waking and sleeping, Thy presence my light.

Be Thou my wisdom, be Thou my true Word;
Be Thou ever with me and I with Thee, Lord;
Be Thou my great Father, and I Thy true son;
Be Thou in me dwelling, and I with Thee one.

Be Thou my breastplate, my sword for the fight;
Be Thou my whole armor, be Thou my true might;

Be Thou my soul's shelter, be Thou my strong tower,
O raise Thou me heavenward, great Power of my power.

I wish you could hear Eden's Bridge perform this song. One woman's voice, soft and clear, her Irish accent peeking out of the vowels, and the patter of palms on simple drums.

Somewhere in the listening I started to cry. These were the good tears that come from joy. There was sadness in the joy because of the longing, but this sadness was rich and sweet.

I stood leaning on a chair and closed my eyes so my ears could have all of me. I ceased all movement so my body could listen. I made myself be the song. I felt the goodness of the words so deeply that my heart broke open and bled joy.

Be Thou my vision . . .
Be all else but naught to me . . .
Be Thou my wisdom, my shelter, my tower.

I wept because I am not my own. I cannot speak to you as a free man. I was raised from childhood to give my life to Christ. Now the profound nature of that giving has become the source of my happiness. How can I separate myself from that which brings joy? Why would I want to?

I could no more leave Christianity than I could shed my own skin. The truth in that song captured me long ago. Deep beauty for me is Christ and the hope of redemption for this world. Yes, THIS world, for I dare not think of the next.

I do not weep for my captivity because I count it as joy.

I know this sounds crazy to many of you. I can't explain it. I'm caught and I want to be caught.

Who am I? They call me Preacher. I am a coarse and common man, a dreamer and a deep feeler. I have never found the sweet spot between raucous laughter and quiet devotion, and I hope I never do. It is good to be ever juggling these virtues.

I am constantly found guilty of the sin of words. Vulgarity is not my downfall, though I am vulgar. My sin is having words that are far more beautiful than my life.

How graceful are those whose lives outshine their words.

Perhaps my life will catch up to my mouth someday. Perhaps my body will catch up to my heart, my hands to my eyes, my feet to my soul.

I have nothing to offer the Creator but myself. Here I am. I have nothing to claim but grace. I want more from life than I deserve and have given back less than I should.

I cannot see the path. I know not the way. I have not avoided the obstacles. Blinded and uncertain, I have only this prayer:

Be Thou my vision.

The Preacher

The advent of Elliot

So what did you do in the '90s?

A couple in our church, Stan and Carol, spent the '90s trying to have a baby. They blew an entire decade doing the infertility dance.

You know the infertility dance, right? First you try to relax and "let it happen." Then you pray to Jesus, who always seems to be busy doing other things. After that you give all your money to doctors and do all the weird shit they recommend. Finally, you bow to your partner and offer up your credit cards.

This dance will flat take it out of you.

None of it worked for Stan and Carol. For them it was just one disappointment after another. Mr. Grief was the only one they could count on. He dropped by once a month to nibble at their souls when they were at their weakest.

They didn't give up; they ran out. They ran out of everything — energy, time, money. They were empty, that's all. They looked to heaven and said, "It is finished." They fell to the dance floor and cried "Uncle."

They tried to hold Mr. Grief at bay, but this was his hour. Denial worked pretty well, some days. Bargaining never did much for them, though some people swear by it. Anger was like heroin — a quick, powerful fix, but anger takes energy and Mr. Grief was patient. In the end, he swept onto the dance floor with a triumphant flourish, and ate them all to pieces.

Our church wore a kind of emotional veil in those days. The light of our joy was always dimmed by their sadness. We rejoiced with every new baby, but couldn't help sneaking a glance at Stan and Carol.

Carol was strong and tried not to show her sadness when new babies came to church. She did pretty good too, but one Sunday she broke down in the parking lot. Stan folded her into their car and mouthed "I'm sorry" to us. They hated to be a bother.

There was nothing you could say. We were walking in darkness with our friends. That's all we could do, just walk in the darkness with them, hoping for some glimmer of light.

The phone call from Yolanda came out of nowhere, and the shock of it caused Carol to sit down hard on the floor. Carol had been one of Yolanda's elementary school teachers. They were close back then and had kept in touch through the years.

Yolanda was pregnant, but wanted to go to college after graduation. She wasn't ready to be a mother. Remembering her beloved teacher and knowing her story, she had a proposition for them. "I thought maybe you guys might want to adopt my baby."

It happened just that quickly. One moment there was nothing but darkness, and the next moment a ray of light.

We were on pins and needles at the church, hungry for every scrap of news and getting updates from Stan and Carol every Sunday. It was absolutely the longest nine months of my life.

And then he came — a little boy with olive skin and dark brown eyes. They named him Elliot. Elliot is his name.

Everything stopped on the Sunday they brought him to church for the first time. We who had walked in darkness saw Stan and Carol coming down the aisle with Elliot. We saw a great light. God, the look in Carol's eyes. Sweet Jesus.

We passed Elliot up and down the rows like a little offering plate, with Stan and Carol standing at the front crying for joy. He bobbed along through the people like a little Moses in the river.

That was a good day.

Carol says God had them wait all those years because God knew Elliot was going to need a family.

That doesn't jibe with my ways of thinking about God, but Carol is expressing things that are beyond language. It's called theology, or God words, and hers make about as much sense as anybody's.

It's been two years now since Elliot has made his way into our world. He's keen on hopping, toy trucks, and "Bob the Builder." He's a bit shy, but is sometimes willing to indulge all the aunts and uncles at church who constantly want hugs and kisses.

He runs up and down the halls of the church on Sundays. He has no idea who he is. He has no idea how long we waited for him.

He's only a little boy, but he's special to us. He brought life to Stan and Carol. He brought them back from the dead. His advent brought light to people who had been walking in darkness.

His name is Elliot. Elliot is his name.

The passion of Elliot

I don't know how the Kramers found our church. We're off the beaten path and we don't advertise. Maybe it was God, I don't know.

Jennifer was only nineteen and David was twenty, but they already looked beaten, worn, and creased. He was a roofer and she worked off and on at the 7-11. Their marriage was shaky at best, and their three-year-old son David Jr. was acting out in ways that one might expect.

This family definitely had some rough edges.

About a month after the Kramers started coming to church we were gathered together for our Wednesday night meal. Everyone was sitting around the tables chatting after supper when we heard a terrible scream from down the hall.

The first thing I saw was Stan and Carol running toward JoAnn, one of our deacons, who was carrying Elliot into the kitchen. He was screaming at the top of his lungs, and there was something in the scream that made every parent stop talking. You knew it was something serious.

Everyone rushed to the kitchen. JoAnn put Elliot on the counter, and people crowded around talking all at the same time. Carol pulled up Elliot's shirt and everyone fell silent. On his back were eight vicious bites, two rows of four oval wounds. The skin was broken and oozing blood. Angry, red welts were rising around the teeth marks.

Do you know the horror that borders on disbelief? Do you know that sad, squinting face people make when they mouth words, but do not say them? That's how we were. The ugliness made us squint. Helpless, we formed words with our mouths, but did not speak.

It was JoAnn who found them in the Sunday school room. David Jr. had dragged Elliot to the ground and was growling as he bit him over and over. Innocent little Elliot, only two years old, didn't even know how to struggle. He was bitten fourteen times, each one drawing blood. He had bites on his back, arms, and head.

As everyone fussed over Elliot, David Jr. walked into the kitchen and watched with an innocent and unconcerned expression. I stared at him in wonder. How can a three-year-old have such rage? How can his anger come and go so quickly? Where did he learn to bite like that?

David and Jennifer came rushing around the corner and immediately saw what had happened. Jennifer cried out, "Oh my God, not again. David!" Then she ran out of the church, crying hysterically.

Later I discovered this was not the first time this had happened. The Kramers had developed a tragic pattern. They would find a church they liked, settle in and begin to make friendships. Then David Jr. would bite a child, forcing them to leave in shame.

They should have warned us, but they were young and foolish. Their denial about their son was only one of the ways they were out of touch with reality.

David picked up his son and pleaded his apologies. As he edged toward the door he kept saying the same thing over and over. "I'm sorry. He knows better. I'm sorry. He knows better."

Tossing one final "I'm sorry" over his shoulder, David ran out the door. I followed him and found Jennifer in the parking lot talking with one of our deacons. I don't know what he was saying to her, but she had a crazy look and was edging toward their old pickup.

I could tell they wanted to leave. Who could blame them? To be honest, I was hoping they *would* leave. I was in such shock. I was trying to be nice, but I was so angry and so sad all at once.

Then the front door of the church banged open and Carol burst out. She ran toward Jennifer who froze and whispered, "Oh my God." As Carol approached, Jennifer lowered her eyes and began to weep and apologize. "I'm so sorry. My God, I'm so sorry."

Carol didn't say anything at first. Then she put her left hand on Jennifer's shoulder and her right hand under her chin. She lifted Jennifer's face and spoke in a very soft, but firm voice. "Stop."

"Listen to me," she said. "Elliot is going to be fine. He will heal, and he will get over this. I'm not worried about Elliot. Do you know what does worry me?"

Jennifer shook her head, tears streaming down her cheeks.

"I'm worried that you and David will be so embarrassed about this that you will never come back to our church. That's the only thing that worries me. We've come to love your family, and you need to be here with us. You need church, and I want you to promise me that you'll come back *this* Sunday."

Jennifer didn't answer her. I don't think she could, really. She did what felt right. She melted into Carol's arms, sobbing. There was something different about the way she was crying, too. It was sad crying, but not as crazy and not as lonely as before.

They stayed like that for a long time, two mothers holding each other in the parking lot. Two mothers crying for their sons.

I watched and had the strangest impulse to take off my shoes.

It's one thing to read about Christ in Bibles and books. It's quite another thing to meet him in person. Quite another thing.

I'll never forget the sight of those horrible wounds on Elliot's little back. They are a stark reminder of the reality of evil and the high price of redemption.

Postscript

The Kramers still attend our church, but not as regularly. We've pushed them to get counseling for their son and their family. We are gentle, but insistent.

When David Jr. is at church, we have an adult who monitors him closely. He seems to be less afraid and has not tried to bite another child.

We are hopeful that in time, they will find healing.

The Preacher

Bifocals

My youngest daughter is the only six-year-old I know who wears bifocals. She has strabismus, which is the doctor's word for crossed eyes. She started wearing glasses at four months and has had a couple of operations along the way.

When you have a child with a difference, that difference becomes part of your love for her.

Her glasses make her eyes look bigger than they really are, giving her a "Hummel" kind of cuteness. If you stand close to her, there is a little magic zone where she isn't sure which lens will best render your face. She will cock her head back to try the bottom lens, then drop her face down and try the top.

I've been known to find this zone and stay there until someone drags me away.

I'm the one who always cleaned her glasses, holding them up to the light, exhaling on them and wiping them with my shirttail. She now does this herself, imitating my every move. She is so serious when she moistens the lenses with her breath, "Hhaa-Hhaa," and wipes them with her shirt.

"Dear Jesus, if you ever show me something sweeter than this child cleaning her little glasses, I might die."

I wish she didn't have a problem with her eyes, but her glasses and all the mannerisms that go with them are a precious part of her. It's a paradox, no doubt about it.

Last Friday she gave the family some good news. "We're having a school holiday for the King who said everyone should get the same."

We didn't know what she was talking about.

My oldest daughter finally figured it out. "She means Martin Luther King Day."

"That's right," she said. "The King who said everyone should get the same."

Oh.

How simply she looks at the world through her tiny lenses, tilting her head to find focus. I will not tell her that we don't live in the King's world, that everyone will not get the same. She will learn this for herself and in her own time.

One day she may find that little cross-eyed girls don't "get the same," and that will be her grief to bear.

She is like her father, is she not? Or am I like her? Cleaning my lenses with my own breath and cloth, tilting my head this way and that, wanting to find focus, hoping to see the good.

We are also alike in that we are very small people in this world. Very small people.

I feel the impulse behind the Hail Mary, spoken by those who do not feel able to pray for themselves.

Holy Mary, mother of God, pray for us sinners.

Pray for us sinners.

The Preacher

The smallest person in all the world

RLPDV

Occasionally I enjoy writing a dramatic version of a story from the Gospels and posting it on my weblog. I have taken to calling these stories "RLPDV," which stands for "Real Live Preacher Dramatized Version."

The name is something of a joke, but I'm very much in earnest about the stories themselves.

The Gospel stories of Jesus are minimal to the point of absurdity. These are skeleton stories, stripped of the flesh of their immediate context. We are not told about the faces or the body language of the characters. In many cases we do not know what happened just before or after the story.

There are good reasons for this. These stories were born of an oral tradition, a tradition of hearing the stories of Jesus told around the fire by those who knew him. The Gospels may have originally served as memory aids in a time when storytelling was still the main way the gospel message was passed along.

Also, paper was expensive and scrolls bulky. It made sense to keep the stories short and let readers fill in the details from their natural understanding of their own culture.

But now many years have passed, and most of us are not familiar with the culture of first-century Palestine. Details that were quite familiar to the original readers must be uncovered and made plain. A little contextual study can make the Gospel stories live and breathe again.

When I write a dramatic version of a Bible story, I am trying to bring these bones to life again. I add details that are reasonable for a first-century culture and combine these details with modern dialogue, so that the characters will seem real.

The details are my own best guesses, but there were real, live details once. There was flesh on the bones of these stories once upon a time, and that makes all the difference.

Part 1: The Rabbi, the Woman, and the Cities

The Rabbi
(Twenty Years Before)

Jesus, son of Joseph, what would you do if you met the smallest person in the world?

The smallest, Rabbi?

Yes, the person who matters the least. The person with absolutely no power. The smallest person in all the world.

How would I know this person, dear Rabbi?

Indeed, how WOULD you know this person? For when we speak of the smallest person in the world we are speaking of the very mathematics of God. It is only with the reckoning of The Almighty that we are able to make sense of a newborn infant, a fallen sparrow, a single hair on your head.

And yet God's math is not known nor can it be found. It can only be received in the instant when it is needed. It exists only in the present moment.

Rabbi, I do not understand.

Young Jesus, you will never understand the mathematics of God until you meet the smallest person in the world and look into her eyes.

The Woman

In the very important city of Tyre, in the bustling and busy center of the business district, slumped against an earthen wall was the smallest person in all the world.

No one knew her name, and no one cared for her. She might have been attractive once, but hard living had taken her softness and left leathery skin, dirty feet, and a wet cough in its place.

Her little girl played at her feet. She was six, but had the mind of a two-year-old. Several times a day she would stiffen and shake with a palsy. Her fingers, wrists, and elbows would draw up, and she would stop breathing. Her face would grow red while spittle bubbled at her lips. In these moments, the woman would hold her and weep while she prayed fervently for the demons to leave her child. Passersby would point and say, "Demons!" They drew their clothing over their mouths and hurried past, terrified.

The woman begged for food in the streets. Pulling her child deep into the folds of her robe, she stretched out a hand to those who walked by. She said nothing for there was nothing to be said. There was no shame in her anymore. Desperation had driven shame away. She looked everyone in the eye and did what she had to do to live and take care of her child.

In the quiet moments of the night, she would look away and remember the man she saw two years before, when her husband, now dead, had taken her to Galilee. There she had seen a miracle worker who was able to cast demons out of children.

They had planned to go back to Galilee and bring their little girl to see Jesus. They had many plans back then, but all that was gone now.

Jesus lived in his world, and she was waiting to die in hers. The smallest person in the world lived each day waiting. She had no hope and nothing to wait for, but she waited all the same.

Waiting was all she had left.

The Cities

"Tyre and Sidon," he said, like it was nothing, like it was no big thing for good Jewish boys to take a little road trip to the "Twin Cities of Sin."

They all laughed because there was no way he was serious, but he kept packing his stuff, and he kept not saying anything. The laughing got quieter and then died out. The disciples started looking uncomfortable. They made eye contact with each other and tried to communicate with exaggerated facial expressions and shoulder shrugs. Several of them caught Peter's eye and indicated with sharp head movements that he should talk to Jesus and find out what the hell was going on.

Peter accepted his appointed role as spokesman without much thought. "Why Tyre and Sidon?"

Jesus never stopped working. He was shoving supplies into a bag, and he spoke without looking up.

"Why not Tyre and Sidon? They've got good accommodations."

The men in the room burst into laughter again. Maybe Jesus was just joking after all. Someone shouted out, "How would YOU know?" and the laughter got even louder.

"I've been there," he said, pulling a rope tight around a bag. He looked up and showed no emotion at all. "I've been there a FEW times."

That silenced everyone. Then Peter put his hand on Jesus' arm and said, "Seriously, why do we need to go . . . there?"

Jesus dropped what he was holding and gave them his full attention.

"Okay guys, here's the deal. I need to get away. Need to get away bad. I need to go somewhere where no one knows me. Understand? I've got a lot of things to tell you, and time is short. Shorter than you know. It seems like we just get started talking and someone comes running up, wanting me to bless a child, or heal their mother-in-law or something. You know how it is.

"I need time alone, just with you. We need to get away and do some serious talking. You don't understand how important our work is, how much is riding on what we do.

"So we're going away. No one will know us, and we can talk in peace. Hey, it'll be fun. Trust me."

*   *   *

Tyre blew their minds. It was big, for one thing. Big and worldly. The chaos and confusion of frenetic commerce was everywhere they looked, from the men on the streets to the people barking from behind fruit stands. And there were women on the street corners too, women of the night.

"Listen now, because this is important. I don't want anyone to know who I am. I do not want to cause a scene. I don't want to teach, preach, or heal anyone. You know how the crowds get out of hand."

Thaddaeus spoke up. "Why not, though? These people need to know God's love, right?" Thaddaeus was like that. Big hearted.

"Yes, Thad, but that is not my calling. My life is given to the children of Israel. It will be for others to bring God's word to the gentiles.

"Have you guys considered what might happen if I healed someone here? Can you imagine if a crowd of needy people followed us home? Can you see me coming back to Capernaum with a mob of lepers and demon-possessed gentiles straggling after me? No. Now is not their time, and everything must be done in its season. Let us use our time here to prepare ourselves for what is to come. Keep your heads down and your noses clean."

Jesus cut right through the center of the city. The streets were very crowded, but he walked with confidence, like a man who knew where he was going. The disciples knotted themselves into a little clump and followed right on his heels, safe in his wake.

"Okay, there are SO many gentiles," Bartholomew said. He was walking with his wrists crossed in front of his chest, moving his shoulders violently to avoid brushing against anyone or anything. "Do you KNOW how unclean we're gonna be?"

Jesus just laughed. He didn't care if he touched a hundred gentiles. He was striding through downtown Tyre like it was his old neighborhood.

"Loosen up, guys. We'll be fine. There are Jewish people here. The Diaspora Jews might be a little scary, but they know how to cook. We'll have soup like your mama makes it tonight; I know a great place. And tomorrow I know a quiet spot where we can talk."

Thaddaeus heard her first. He was in the back of the group, and he was feeling vulnerable. He had already stepped on the heel of James's sandal twice because he was trying to stay close behind him. James was getting pissy about it, so Thaddaeus was looking down, watching where he put his feet when he heard the faintest sound over the noises of the city. It sounded like a woman's voice from far away. It sounded like she shouted, "Jesus."

Thaddaeus stopped and turned around. He scanned the street, but all he saw were people moving fast and in every direction. "Nah," he said as he turned and trotted to catch up with the group.

Then he heard it again, this time louder.

"Jesus! Hey Jesus! Jeeee-suuuus!"

Part Two: The Voice, the Eyes, and the Math of God

The Voice

This time they all heard it. Jesus stopped abruptly, and some of the disciples bumped into him. They turned around and looked down the street, trying to find the voice.

"Jesus, son of David. Have mercy on me. Jesus!"

All their heads snapped to the right a little, and then they saw her, back thirty paces or so, across the road. A ragged looking woman yelling loudly and waving her hand. She was working against the flow of human traffic, trying to cross the road at an angle to catch up with them. It was hard to tell, but it looked like she was dragging a child behind her.

"Keep walking," said Jesus, turning quickly and heading away. She saw them leaving, and her shouts grew louder and more frantic.

"Jesus, stop! Please, come back. Have mercy on me, son of David. Oh please! It's not for me, it's for my baby!"

People started paying attention. Following her gestures, a few even pointed at Jesus and the disciples who were obviously trying to get away from her.

Peter worked his way up to Jesus.

"Listen, man, you gotta do something about this woman. She's starting to make a scene, which is exactly what you didn't want. How does she know you anyway? What does she want?"

Jesus looked pained. "I know what she wants, but I can't give it to her. We can't do our work here. I am only called to work among the children of Israel. I have to follow the rules on this one, Peter. I have to. Everything could be at risk."

"Hey, man," said Peter. "You don't have to convince me. I never wanted to come to this God-forsaken place anyway."

The crowd thinned a little, and Jesus was able to walk more quickly.

When she saw that she was losing them, she cried out one last time. She reached down into her soul and found the ancient sound of sorrow. This sound is the birthright of every mother, and it carries great power. It cannot be faked or easily ignored.

"No, Jesus. Stop!"

The sound of sorrow was her last move and her only hope. She hurled it at Jesus with all her might. Her voice hit him like a fist in the back, stiffening him and stopping him in his tracks. He was not able to walk, but he didn't turn around. He just stood there, facing away from her, head down, breathing hard. The disciples milled around him, wondering what happened.

She came a little closer, but tentatively, scared she might frighten him away. She spoke again, but softer. "Please, I call out to you in the name of God. Son of David, please, help my little girl."

Peter grabbed Jesus by the arm. "What are you doing? Why are you stopping?"

Jesus looked at Peter, amazed. "You heard the sound of that voice. How are you able to walk away?"

He turned to face the woman, now only ten steps behind them. She stood still, panting and watching them. She seemed shocked that they had actually stopped.

Jesus spoke softly to the disciples. "I'm going to tell her the truth. She deserves that much."

"What do you mean, the truth?" asked James.

"I mean the truth. I'm going to tell her exactly why I cannot heal her daughter.

"I'm going to tell her what our people think of her people. And she's going to hate me. She will absolutely hate me, but hating me is better than her thinking that her daughter isn't worth healing."

The Eyes

The woman walked to Jesus with her little girl in front of her. Then she knelt before him. And there she was, the sum of all their fears. A gentile. Unclean. Needy. A distraction, a bother, a problem.

"Jesus of Nazareth, I know you. I saw you two years ago. I know that you have the power of God. Please, heal my little girl. We don't ask much. My husband is dead, and I am reduced to begging, but that's okay. I can live with that if only you will make her well. She's so little and she doesn't even know how hard her life will. . . . Just please, make her well. I know you can."

She fell silent, then bowed her head and waited.

Jesus paused, and this moment seemed like an eternity. The crowd moved around them, but some curious onlookers stopped to see what was going on.

It was a hard call to make, but it was Jesus' call, and he made it. He made the call back when he first heard her, and he wasn't going to back away from his decision now.

"I'm sorry. I truly am sorry, but I cannot do this for you. I know you will not understand, but I cannot take what is meant for God's children, and give it to the dogs."

Jesus never took his eyes off the woman. He swallowed hard and waited for her anger.

But her anger never came. Not one hint of anger crossed her face. She was a mother with a sick child. She was beyond anger, beyond reason, and beyond desperation. You could insult her, strike her, spit in her face, and she would only be thinking about how she might get you to help her child.

She did not get angry; she got stronger. She rose to her feet with a dignity that surprised them all, even Jesus. She pulled her chin up with pride and looked right into his eyes. And then she had her say.

"I know how you

feel about us. I've been to Galilee. That's where I saw you. 'Galilee of the Gentiles,' you call it, but I could tell that people despised me even there.

"You say that you are the chosen people of God. Maybe you are. Maybe compared to you we seem like dogs. I know life isn't exactly great in these parts, but let me tell YOU something. Around here, we save a few scraps to feed the puppies under the table, you know? We might not know that much about God, but we know something about compassion.

"See, there you stand, an important rabbi with a powerful history, but you don't even have scraps for someone like me. I think maybe you should ask yourself just what it means to BE God's chosen people."

Jesus was stunned by her words, and then wonder flooded his face. He bent closer and looked deeply into her eyes.

"Do I know you?" he asked.

And then he saw it. She had the rabbi's eyes. Same color, same shape, same gentle honesty. She was not condemning him; she was seeing him and speaking the truth to him.

"Rebbi," he whispered.

The Math of God

At that instant, in a flash of enlightenment, Jesus understood the mathematics of God. In that moment it was given that he should stand outside of time and know a deeper truth. Sometimes it is right that everything should stop for the smallest person in all the world. Sometimes one person is worth as much as all the people. Sometimes the least is the greatest and the first is the last.

And maybe, in just the right moment, one person could carry the sin of the world on his shoulders.

"I understand," he said to no one in particular.

The math of God filled his soul, and the beauty of it, the unexplainable beauty, welled up inside of him, driving a shiver up his spine. A smile burst onto his face. He laughed out loud and put his palm on her cheek.

"Woman, I had no idea. I didn't know such faith existed outside of my own people. I did not know until now. Yes, absolutely. What you want will be done for you."

He bent and held the little girl's head between his hands. He kissed her forehead, holding his lips there for a moment. Her eyes closed, and then he drew back. When her eyes opened again, he saw that she had the eyes of the rabbi, just like her mother, full of intelligence and curiosity.

Jesus took one look at her, smiled, and walked away. The disciples were stunned and trailed after him. They did not know what they had seen.

The smallest woman in all the world held her child, looked into her eyes, and let out a shout. People parted around Jesus as he moved away, then melted back together as he passed through. By the time she looked up, Jesus was gone forever.

No one said anything for a few minutes. They walked in silence. The disciples could tell that something important had happened, but they weren't sure what it was, exactly.

It was Jesus who spoke first. "I think we have about a half an hour to get out of town before people start looking for me. Let's go home, whaddya say?"

Several nodded their agreement, but Thaddaeus spoke up. "What about the retreat? What about all those things you said you needed to teach us?"

Jesus laughed and put both hands on Judas's shoulders from behind, leaning on him and letting Judas pull him along for a step or two. Then he let go and punched Peter on the shoulder.

"I think we've learned enough for one day."

Note: This story occurs in two places in the gospels. Mark's account gives us the clue that Jesus did not want to be recognized. Matthew's account shows us how Jesus struggled within himself and the wonderful interaction he had with the disciples.
Mark 7:24-30
Matthew 15:21-28

The Preacher

Vision on Comanche Hill

Rising from the middle of the suburbs in our town is a wild and lonely hill called Comanche Hill. Strangely out of place among the tract homes and schools, it has gone undeveloped and is still covered with live oak, ashe juniper, huisache, and other South Texas plants. My favorite is the enticing agarita, a wild holly bush with yellow berries that make a wonderful jelly.

Native American people once used this hill for its stunning and strategic view of an ancient trail that lies at its base. That trail is currently a paved thoroughfare, but was once a Spanish "highway," and before that was a major trail for Native American tribes moving across the land we now call Texas.

They considered this hill to be a sacred place of vision and visions. Its vantage point allowed them to spot their enemies while they were yet far away. From this hill they saw their future and changed the present to prepare for what was to come.

Apparently Comanche Hill still has some of that old magic because I had a powerful and life-changing vision there while hiking with two of my daughters.

Hiking is a big deal in our family. I've outfitted the three sisters with backpacks and the kind of adventure kits you can assemble for about ten bucks at a discount store.

- A small hammer.
- A screwdriver to be used as a chisel.
- A paintbrush for delicate "archaeology" work.
- Band-Aids.

- Tweezers.
- Little plastic bottles for storing specimens.
- Candy.

The day I received my vision we parked on a suburban street before ascending Comanche Hill. The contrast was disorienting. Every step up felt like a step back in time. If the change of scenery was my peyote, the girls' chatter was my mantra.

"Dad, what are these flowers called?"

"Flowers don't really have names. What do YOU want to call them?"

"Can I call them "Little Purple Sweet Tarts"?

"Daddy, see this rock? I found it. Only when I found it, it was under another rock so I had to dig them both out of the ground."

Both girls are keen on digging for fossils and arrowheads. The middle one is careful, brushing away dirt from the rocks she hopes are fossils but never are. The youngest one is more into speed digging. She chisels away at the ground with her hammer and screwdriver.

"Hey, I think I found an arrowhead," she said, lifting a flattish river rock from the ground.

We were making our way to the top of the hill when it happened. I was walking behind them on the trail when the vision came.

There is a beautiful time in the life of a little girl when her bottom is so tiny you can't believe it. She gallops around on coltish legs and slightly oversized feet. It's an age of dirty shoes and skinned knees. She's awkward, but her hands are growing delicate and nimble. She dots her i's with hearts and loves purple ink. She won't wash her hair, but she begins to linger at the closet, wondering what to wear.

She wants womanly things, but doesn't know what to do with them. She covets makeup, but can't apply it. She begs for a diary then fills it with pictures of horses and rainbows. She is betwixt and between. She is neither here nor there.

And she wants to be with her dad more than anything in the whole wide world.

Be still my heart.

It's a delicate stage and fleeting. You can miss it in the blink of an eye.

This I know from experience. My oldest daughter is fourteen and wasn't with us on this day. She had other things to do. Her hiking days aren't over, but she doesn't bring her backpack anymore. Her interests are beginning to turn.

My vision was a simple one. In a flash I knew what was walking right in front of me. We all think we know what we want. We definitely know what we've had and lost. To know what you have is the rare gift.

It's not foresight or hindsight we need. We need sight, plain and simple. We need to see what is right in front of us.

There is only a narrow slice of my life where I get to do this. There is only a small window of time for pink backpacks, "Little Purple Sweet Tarts," and pretend arrowheads.

And even now I hear the distant voice of the auctioneer, shouting, "Going, going, GONE!"

On Saturday I saw my enemy. I named him and gained power over him. He was close enough for me to count coup. He is always with me. The enemy is not the aging of my children. Their growth is a good thing and will bring new joys along the way.

I am the enemy. Sometimes I don't know what I have until it becomes what I had.

The vision came in an instant, as visions do. I had a digital camera, so I snapped a quick picture of them walking ahead of me on the trail. I stopped to stare at the image, and when I looked up they were already far in front of me, moving up and away.

I had to run to catch them. I was trying to look at the incredible picture on the camera screen while stumbling over rocks. All of a sudden *I* was the awkward one, bumping along while shoving things back into my backpack. I shouted up the trail.

I wanted them to slow down and wait for me.

The Preacher

The three sisters

In 1997 I could not read the stars. I recognized no human track or sign in the night sky. I saw the heavens with the eyes of a child.

Our third daughter was born that winter. We had decided three was our limit, so I was not going to have the son I had dreamed of. Those were strange days because I experienced grief and joy in equal measures. I had a vision of a little boy with a baseball glove who hung his head and turned away from me.

One night I noticed three little stars all in a row. I stopped and stared. "The Three Sisters," I whispered to myself. I had another vision, this time of three women meeting for tea. They stopped their conversation and smiled at me.

In those days I went outside almost every night to look at The Three Sisters. I began to notice a red star that was always in a different place in the sky. It seemed to move across the constellations, on a journey all its own. I puzzled over this. Something seemed sad about the little star with no home. I began calling it "The Little Lost Boy."

Every night The Little Lost Boy moved closer to the horizon. I hated to see him go, but eventually I had to say goodbye. And so I did.

My stargazing was so innocent in those days — so childlike and so helpful to me.

Then I bought The Audubon Society's *Field Guide to the Night Sky*. I pored over it and discovered that what I was calling "The Three Sisters" was really Orion's belt. I also found that "The Little Lost Boy" was Mars. The planets do not have a set location in the sky, but seem to move in and out of the constellations. He wasn't lost at all.

The winter constellations became known to me, and I counted them as friends. Orion the strong with Lepus the hare at his feet and red-eyed Taurus over his shoulder. The teacup Pleiades, faithful Canis Major and the watchful Gemini twins. Capella the she-goat with her three kids. Leo the lion rising in the east to chase them all away.

I wanted to know these things. I wanted to read the human language of the constellations. I gained knowledge, and the knowledge was good.

I also lost something. Had I known the constellations, I never would have seen The Three Sisters and The Little Lost Boy. I would have never found that gentle path through and beyond my sadness.

The fruit of the tree of knowledge nourishes the soul, but it has a price. Once you have tasted it, you can never see with the eyes of a child again.

Pick up a book and look at the letters. You cannot see them as a child sees them. As soon as you look at the page, the letters will group themselves into words and phrases. They seem to have a life of their own. Once we come to understand these symbols, they are forever imprinted upon us. Our mind is molded by our knowledge.

Here's something fun. Turn the book upside down and look at the letters. It's like becoming a child again.

I cannot turn the sky upside down. The constellations jump into my vision and the planets are not as mysterious now that I know their names. In some ways the stars are closed to me now. I read them better, but they speak to me less.

There are nights when I look at the sky and wish I did not know. I wish I could find The Little Lost Boy, but he is gone forever, swallowed up by Mars.

I'm intrigued by this finding and losing. I wonder about this trade-off between knowledge and vision, this price we pay to read our world.

Jesus said, "Unless you become like a child, you will never enter the Kingdom of Heaven."

I stand in my yard and speak to the sky. "What did you mean by that, Jesus?

"Why would you ask something so impossible of me?"

The Preacher

Between hope and memory

I'm interested in memory because memory is all we have. We are unable to perceive the temporal singularity of the present, which is a razor-sharp edge. It cuts our experience into past and future. We understand the division, but cannot comprehend the blade.

I have nothing but my own quickly fading memories out of which to build my reality. These memories lose focus and detail as they disappear behind me, drifting far into the past.

How hopefully I bind them together even as they fall apart. How boldly I proclaim reality even as I forget it.

We live in the transition between the future and the past. We are the moment that hope becomes memory.

Someday I will be dead and my children will cobble together their ragged memories and create me anew. They will create me in their own image. I will be clay in their hands with only the breath of their memories to give me life.

So I spend a fair amount of energy trying to create good memories for my three daughters. This may seem rather contrived, but I'm of the opinion that parenting is mostly contrived. There's really no time for much else.

Plant good memories while you can, mommies and daddies. Our time on earth is short and hope becomes remembrance in the twinkle of a little girl's eye.

AD 2063

A seventy-year-old woman points her grandson's hand toward the eastern sky on a November evening. Orion's belt of three stars hangs low near the horizon, forming a nearly perfect vertical line.

"The middle star, that one's mine. Its name is Alnilam. That means 'string of pearls.' My father gave me that star because I was his middle daughter. He said I was his string of pearls."

She stares at the star and tilts her head slightly. "I was his string of pearls."

"What about the other stars, Grandma Shelby?"

"Well, the top star is Reiley's. She was the oldest. The last star is Lillian's because she was the baby. Each year they rise in the east, just in the order we were born. See?

"Most people call it Orion's belt, but Daddy always called it 'The Three Sisters.' He said he had as much a right to name the stars as anyone. He used to say, 'Look for The Three Sisters in November, when I am gone.

"'Look to the sky and remember that you were loved.'"

The Preacher

Everett Joseph Smith was a real boy

The phone call came at night. Doesn't it seem like they always do? I felt sick. I hung up the phone and turned to my wife. "John and Denise's baby came."

There was nothing to say, really. We sat there feeling horror and dread. "How far along?" she asked.

"Twenty-two weeks. A little boy, and he was alive."

Her face fell. My wife is a chaplain. She spent years working labor and delivery, so she knows what twenty-two weeks means.

At twenty weeks, he would have been born dead. At twenty-five weeks he would have had a fighting chance. Twenty-two weeks is just old enough for the heart to beat but too young for the lungs to breathe.

Twenty-two weeks.

John and Denise lost a little girl the same way a few years back. She just came too soon. Everyone who knew them saw how scared they were this time. We were counting the weeks, hoping and praying it wouldn't happen again. But it did.

Twenty-two weeks.

I gathered my keys and wallet and put a small New Testament into my pocket. "I've got to go to the hospital, but there's something important I want to ask you before I go."

I asked. She thought a moment and gave me her answer. It was the right answer, but it was a little scary. It put some pressure on me.

"Okay," I said and got into my car.

When you are the pastor of a church, you are many things. You are an agent of grace and hope, a repository of spiritual and scriptural wisdom, and a gatekeeper at big events like weddings and funerals. Somehow people weave all of these into a complex image of you. You are all things to all people.

And sometimes you are the Black Rider of Death. People indulge in all sorts of denial while they are waiting for the minister. It's a blessed procrastination that helps them make it for a short time. And then you appear, framed in the hospital doorway, Bible in hand.

I am come. Let the grieving begin.

When I got to Denise's room, I could tell they were waiting for me. I saw a little boy in a shallow tray under a light. He had no covers or clothes, and he was shockingly small. Stunning in his smallness. You would stare if you saw him. Denise was quiet in her bed. Some of her family were with her along with a woman from our church who is one of her closest friends. One or two of them rose to their feet when I appeared at the door.

I am a keeper of a most sacred truth. It is the incarnation truth that enables ministers to walk into the grief storm unafraid. If you come in the name of Christ and stand with people in their grief, you have done the most important thing you can do and the only thing they will remember. You might bring words with you, and they might even be good and helpful ones, but your presence is what matters.

If you know this truth, whatever you have will be sufficient. If you do not know this, all that you have will not be enough.

I went straight to Denise's bed. She began to tremble a little in anticipation of grief as I approached. I put my arms around her and let my cheek touch the side of her head. I spoke to her in a soft voice. "I come in the name of the Lord who has not forsaken you."

And so it began.

She who felt forsaken by everyone and everything, especially God, burst asunder, and her grief came rushing down like a mighty stream, filling every low place. Hers was a mother's grief. She wrapped her sorrow around her bicep like an addict and pulled it tight with her teeth. Then she sliced her moorings and delivered herself unto her mourning. We lashed ourselves to her bed and held on for dear life.

She did a lightning round of grief stages, raging at God and at her own body. She wept, she denied, she pleaded, she gave in. She talked to her little boy. She apologized for not having a better womb, for not being able to hold him. She said she was sorry so many times that it became pathetic, and we hung our heads in shame for hearing it.

It was hard labor, this grief, and it came in howling waves. At times we hung onto the bed like people holding onto a lamppost in a tornado, and our feet would be lifted from the ground. In these moments we lived only in the present. We had no thought for the morrow, but only wondered how we might hang on a little longer.

When she rested, our feet would settle back to the ground, and we would shift them and stretch our backs, waiting for the next blast.

John grieved like many men I know. He kept his sorrow locked away and busied himself with caring for her. He hovered over the bed, whispering words of encouragement and fluffing her pillow. She was the voice, the oracle, the truth teller for the family. He left the gift of his care at her altar and stood back to watch the words issue forth from the darkness.

I looked at him sadly, for I know that grief abides no proxies. Sorrow will come for him some dark night when he is alone, and on that night there will be no one to speak for him. Grief can be terrible that way.

But this is how they grieved, and it was good enough. They got down to the business of it, and I was honored to bear witness.

There came a time when Denise rested, and I walked over to look at the little boy in the tray. He was about ten inches long, a Barbie doll with an apple-sized head. His skin was waxy and almost transparent. His eyes were sealed shut like a newborn puppy. He looked like a boy, but there was something alien about him. He was not ready for this world.

He was born with a heart that was ready and able, though. You could see it beating through the translucent skin of his chest, faithfully doing its part. There was something innocent and hopeful about his heart. It looked like a baby salmon fluttering in a yolk sack, ready to be born. It was like a child knocking at the door, wanting to come out and play.

But you cannot play without lungs, and his weren't ready. All he was granted were a few precious moments to struggle and reach for life. When the umbilical cord was cut he had no oxygen, and his body lost whatever strength it had. He settled back and gave up the fight, but his heart throbbed for almost two hours. It was a sad reminder of what might have been.

I was afraid to touch him. He was so limp and delicate, like wet cookie dough. It seemed like he would come apart if you tried to pick him up, but John held him with no fear. He wrapped him in a blanket and held him like any baby should be held. When John lifted him, his head lolled back and his mouth popped open. In that moment I felt a stab of knowledge that hurt me.

This is a real boy.

They told me they named him Everett Joseph Smith, and they seemed glad that he had a name.

Before I left my house that evening I asked my wife one question. "I know that being there in the name of Christ is the main thing, but is there anything else I can do for them?"

This is what she said:

"If you can, find a way to make their goodbye memorable. They need to remember that he was real. In the coming days, many of their friends and family will want to pretend that this child never existed. They will want to gloss over the reality of his life in an attempt to ease their pain. Don't be a part of that. All they will ever have is the memory of this goodbye, so make it the best goodbye you can."

I asked John if I could hold his son, and he let me. He was so light, no heavier than the blanket, really. I kissed his head and noticed that it was already cold. His heart was slowing down, barely beating. I took a chance and said, "Would you like to say a goodbye prayer with your son while his heart still beats?"

My question kicked off a new round of crying, and for a moment I wondered if what I said was too much for them. But they were holding each other while they cried, and they nodded. They did want to pray with him.

Denise's prayer was like some I've read in the book of Psalms. She was passionate in her praying, accusing and confessing and finally weeping. It was an honest prayer and good. John held his son in his arms and prayed the sweetest whisper prayer I've ever heard.

After the wrenching labor of this terrible grief, I think it was John who gave birth to hope.

This is what he said:

"Dear God, thank you for our lives. Thank you for my son, even if we only had him for a little while. Take him to be with his sister, and watch over them both so we can meet them someday. Help me and Denise as we try to get through this."

After a few minutes the nurse came, and we noticed that his heart had finally stopped. She gravely put her stethoscope to his chest and pronounced that it was finished. They swaddled him in a blanket, put him in a little basket, and then he was gone.

One by one we left to go home and rest. For John and Denise, the long journey of grief was just beginning.

Looking back on that night, there are two things I want to say.

I say that grief is a painful labor, but hope may be born of sorrow. Be honest with your grief. Keep your eyes open so you won't miss the moment when hope appears.

I say that.

And I say that Everett Joseph Smith was a real boy.

The Preacher

You ain't Jesus, Preacher

Part 1: The Tower of Babel

Everyone has identity issues now and again. Maybe you don't know who you are or don't like who you think you might be. Maybe you're a little too close to your mother, or maybe you live vicariously through your children. Maybe you think you're Clint Eastwood or wish you were Jennifer Lopez.

The point is we all have times when we're not sure who we are. It's a human thing.

I HAVE noticed that most people do not think they are Jesus. There's Jesus Christ, who lived two thousand years ago, and there's you. My guess is you're having no trouble keeping this straight in your mind. Am I right?

So why is it ministers have trouble with this? Have you noticed how many ministers think they're Jesus? How grandiose is that? The minister can't have normal issues like everyone else, oh no. If the preacher is going to get enmeshed with someone, it's going to be with the Lord Jesus Christ himself.

I'm serious now. We need a twelve-step program.

"Hi. My name is Pastor Pete, and I think I'm Jesus."

(All together now) "Hi, Pastor Pete!"

I know a lot about this because I'm a minister, and sometimes I think I am Jesus. Not all the time, mind you, but sometimes I do. I've gotten better over the years. Sometimes I think I'm over it, but then I fall off the wagon and start thinking I'm Jesus again.

I have a problem. I hear admitting your problem is the first step toward healing. I hope that's true.

Why don't I tell you the story of how ministers come to think they're Jesus and what happens when they hit bottom.

It all starts so innocently.

First, you decide that you're not going to be that cheesy minister with the expensive suits and the store-bought smile. You're not going to work the room, tossing hugs and lovey-dovey words into the crowd like Mardi Gras beads. You want real relationships. You're not going to call all the little boys "bearcat" and all the little girls "cutie-pie." You will know the children as individuals. You will know all their names.

Then you decide you're going to be "authentic." What you mean is that you intend to tell the truth. You aren't going to sling bullshit religious slogans around. You aren't going to give easy answers. You aren't going to worry about whether you sound conservative or liberal. You'll take whatever comes your way as a result.

You also want to be just the bestest pastor ever. You want to be insightful and wise, but tastefully self-deprecating. You will work very hard to preach good sermons, but at the same time you won't take them too seriously. You plan to challenge without judging and inspire without seeming inspirational. You will be smart, well-read, and articulate, but you'll only let the hem of those garments show.

Finally, you decide that you want to love everyone, even the visitors. You watch the room to make sure that no one is left alone. You will drop anything to talk to anyone. All they have to do is call you, and everyone has your number. Love is the main thing, and you hope that God might seem real to people because your love was real to them.

You're serious, too. Really. You're not false about this stuff. You are a lot of things, but false and manipulative you are not. You don't want money. You don't want fame. You just want to make God happy and be there to help people on their journey to discovering God.

See how it happens? See? You're going to be everyone's servant, and your love will bring people back to God. Suddenly, you're Jesus. You had the best of intentions, but good intentions don't mean shit if you start thinking you're Jesus.

The crazy thing is, it's the good ministers who end up thinking they're Jesus. The TV preachers who are trying to get your money and the fancy ministers who are building little kingdoms for themselves — they know they aren't Jesus. Everyone knows they aren't Jesus. Look at their haircuts, for pity's sake.

No, it's the good guys who fall into this trap.

And it IS a trap, because I got news for you, Preacher. You ain't Jesus, and you better figure that out right quick.

Part 2: Losing the Language of Love

This is the story of how ministers find out they're not Jesus. This is the story of hitting bottom.

You start figuring out you're not Jesus when you begin to unravel and lose the details. And if you've fallen into the trap of thinking you're Jesus, there are a lot of details to keep straight.

One day your act starts to fray around the edges.

There's the family whose son is in jail. Did you send that letter to the chaplain? Clay seems depressed again. When was the last time you had lunch with him? Remember that little girl who told you she wished you were her daddy? Weren't you going to do some serious thinking about how to respond to her?

Did you pick up that book for Susan's husband, like you said you would? He doesn't feel at home at church. A little gesture like that could mean a lot. Hey, remember Bob and Linda? Jim's children? They haven't been to church in quite a while. They were moving to Hondo, right? Or did Jim say they weren't moving after all? Holy Shit, you forgot to call Kay. Her grandmother is sick, and her mother just died. How could you not call her?

Is that wedding THIS week? What's the groom's last name again? Did you visit Joan in the hospital? She was there for three days. Wasn't there a little girl who wanted to talk to you? Weren't you going to have lunch with . . . um . . . that one guy?

The voices in your head come together as one pounding headache of an entity and name themselves Legion. The details are knotted into a dirty crowd, like starving kids on TV. There are so many of them, each precious, and you aren't keeping up.

You CAN'T keep up, but you MUST keep up, because how can you NOT keep up?

You swear to God that you'll try harder, but God doesn't want that oath. God wants you to find a quiet place, sit down, and remember who you are.

But you want to try harder, because down inside you think you're supposed to be like Jesus. So God stands aside and lets you have your way. The details rush into the void like giggling demons, and everything starts to fall apart.

Calendars blur before your eyes and become your greatest enemy. You know you wrote something down in a Monday square, but later it's in a Friday square. You would swear on a stack of Bibles that there is another week this month, but there isn't. All the weeks are gone, Preacher. Time's up, and you're on. Weddings and speaking engagements skate furiously out of the distant future, pulling up short on the tomorrow square, spraying ice in your eyes.

Even your beloved words begin to fail you.

The blessing you have quoted every Sunday for eight years disappears from your mind without a trace, leaving you speechless before the congregation.

The people at church think your absentmindedness is kind of cute. Maybe they think that's what comes with a creative personality. You hope they think that. You wonder if something might be wrong with your brain.

You develop a little tick. You start needing to squeeze your eyes shut tightly and jerk your head to the side. It occurs to you that it must look like you're saying, "NO!" You consider seeing a doctor, but that's another detail you leave hanging.

Then one Sunday a woman raises her hand in church to share a prayer request. You know this woman. You were there the night her baby was born dying. You held his premature body and watched his final heartbeats through the waxy skin of his tiny chest. YOU KNOW THIS WOMAN. You know her husband and their boy, but her name is gone from your mind. Her name is nowhere. The pause gets too long so you just point at her, and she knows you forgot her name. You can see it in her eyes; you can see it hurt her. She's the saddest person in the world, and you hurt her.

Grief seizes your chest, and all your energy drains into your shoes. You want to stop in the middle of the service, take a seat in the pew and say, "Someone take over. I can't preach or pray or talk. Someone put your arms around me because I can't do anything."

But you don't do that. You don't want to let everyone down, so you dig deep and find energy in a secret place. The price of this energy is putting the woman out of your mind. It's a terrible price to pay. It's a quick fix, but in the long run you lose your soul.

This is what you've come to. Putting people out of your mind so you can finish the sermon. Is this what you call love, Preacher?

You see, when you start forgetting blessings and names, you've lost the language of love. You can forget a lot of things, but you cannot forget a woman's name and claim to love her. You cannot.

You tried to build a tower to the heavens, so God took away your words. It had to be this way. This was the only way you would learn.

Now you understand. You're not Jesus after all. You're a man who is good with words and who feels things very deeply. You're a dreamer and a silly person, like all the other silly people at church. You cannot love everyone, and you cannot be all things to all people.

Welcome to the human race, Preacher. Now you're ready to begin.

You will love some people deeply. Others will receive lesser kinds of love. Some will get a handshake and a kind word. Their journeys are their own, and they may have to get what they need from someone else.

Love the ones you can. Touch the ones you can reach. Let the others go. If you run out of gas, sit down in the pew and point to God. That might be the greatest sermon you ever preach.

You can't love anyone until you understand that you can't love everyone.

You can't be a real live preacher until you understand that you're only a real live person.

The Preacher

Just to sit and cry and not be bothered

Things are pretty quiet in the mountain town of Creede, Colorado. You will not find fast food or fast living there. If you want someone to package your entertainment and provide it with instructions, you should probably go elsewhere. Nothing is franchised in Creede, not the stores or even the churches.

It's the mountain way.

That's why my family goes to Creede every summer. We go for the mountains and because we enjoy not being told how to have fun.

We always stop by the Ramble House on Main Street, a kind of fishing and mercantile establishment. I'm sad to tell you that Alvin died a few years back. His seat is still there by the fireplace where he held court, tying flies and sharing his wisdom. Back in the day, you could talk with Alvin while your kids ate popcorn and looked at the toys and moccasins on the back wall.

Jim and Susan's bead shop is in the white house down from the gas station. That's their dog Sam on the front porch. He's friendly. You can get everything you need there for a night of jewelry-making with your children.

And make sure you stop by the ranger station. The ranger on duty will take the kids to the back room to see the stuffed bear and give them a bag of key chains, rulers, coloring books, and whatever else happens to be on hand. Each child may also select one nature poster from the wooden cabinet with all the drawers.

My girls and I always speculate as to how that one ranger lost a chunk out of his ear. They spin wild tales, but I always stick with the same one-word explanation: "Badger." We haven't worked up the courage to ask him what really happened.

Now in the center of this little village sits a tiny church that I love as much as any place in the whole world. Every year I sit on the back row, hoping to find worship for myself. And every year I cry through the entire service. I'll tell you why in a moment.

They call themselves "Creede Community Church." I believe they are a United Church of Christ congregation, but their minister is a Methodist circuit rider like in the old days. It's a mountain church in a mountain town, and you get the feeling that religious affiliations don't mean as much when you live so close to the timber line.

The minister preaches early Sunday morning down the mountain somewhere, perhaps in South Fork. Then he heads upriver to preach at Creede. He is not slick. His clothes are, shall we say, practical. His sermons are wonderful but perhaps lack some of the polish that can be had for those willing to pay the high price that comes with that sort of nonsense.

The worship service isn't slick either. Most everything is done by volunteers. The six or eight people who make up the choir fuss with their sheet music and await the exaggerated "one, two, three, four" from the music leader before belting out a hymn or two. The pianist also organizes the Vacation Bible School and stands right at the piano to announce that they need toilet paper tubes and macaroni for art projects. People are directed to leave these items in a box in the foyer.

I'm telling you, this is one of the greatest places on earth.

The first time I went to this church, I eased myself into a pew like a man slipping into a warm bath. "Thank God I don't have to do anything," I said to myself. The minister came to the pulpit in an inexpensive suit with a tie that just almost matched. Just, mmm . . . that close to matching. I think he was wearing hiking boots.

When he opened his mouth I began to cry, and I never stopped crying until the service was over.

That first year a few kind souls in the back certainly noticed the stranger who cried through the whole service. One woman offered me tissues. But in the fashion of the Lord's most experienced servants, they left me alone. They could see that something was going on between me and God, and they were pleased to play their part. Their part was to nod kindly, hand over the tissues, and give me a place just to sit and cry and not be bothered.

They are a mountain church and a mountain people. Mountains, by and large, let people be, and they do the same. Thank the Lord for tender mercies.

I go back every year, and the same thing happens. I bring my own tissues now. A pocketful will do. When the service starts I begin crying softly, and I pretty much cry straight through to the end. Then I leave. They let me come and go in peace. They trust that I will ask if I need something more.

They have no idea why I'm crying, of course, and I didn't know myself that first year. I'm not certain even now, but I have some ideas.

I cry in their church because I can't cry in my own. I'm not suggesting that we discourage crying at our church. I'm saying I am not ABLE to cry there. Being in charge shuts something down in me, I think. So every summer in Creede I unpack a year's worth of sorrow, joy, and wonder.

I cry in their church because it is my turn to be served. I'm like the woman who prepares the meals for her family each day. One day she comes home, and her children have prepared a meal for her. She bursts into tears because it's her turn to receive. It doesn't mean she wants to stop cooking. It's just nice that it's her turn.

I cry for those reasons, but mostly I cry because at Creede Community Church I can see the truth. Sitting in that simple pew on the back row, I see the Church Universal in all her glory and silliness. The truth is, we are not sophisticated at all. We are nothing more than children, sticking our drawings to the fridge with tiny magnets, offering our best to the heavens on a wing and a prayer. We are precious, but perhaps only in His sight.

With my eyes closed, it almost seems like my feet don't touch the floor. I become like a child in my Father's house. My weakness is known to me, but I am okay with weakness. I know my place. I see myself as one child among many, bowing my head seriously, but not realizing that I have a milk moustache and my shoes are on the wrong feet.

I think messy little boys and girls praying in church must be irresistible to God. When God slows down and licks his fingers to slick down my cowlick, I catch a fleeting glimpse of the hem of his robe.

And a glimpse is more than enough for me.

That is the moment of true worship, and I always seem to find it in Creede.

And in that moment, I cry from pure joy and relief.

The Preacher

Goodbye, Daddy

I was not involved in the world of weblogs before I began Real Live Preacher, so I was surprised when I discovered the intimacy and passion of the communities that form around various blogs. The comments left at Real Live Preacher are the tangible expression of one of these communities. Frequently the comments take on a life of their own. People respond to each other, comfort one another, and sometimes share their own writing.

When I wrote this essay I had a strong sense that the readers of Real Live Preacher would join me in praying for Chris. I received numerous emails and comments that confirmed this. The next time I saw "Chris" at church, I told her that many people were praying for her and thinking about her in her grief. I think it meant a great deal to her.

My friend Christina sent me a very short email on Monday. Four words. "My daddy is dead."

That was all she said, and it was all she had to say. Chris is a poet; she's used to letting a few words tell her story. You can understand or not understand. She's fine either way.

Poets are strong like that.

I understood. I know about the rainy night her mother pushed her down into the tall grass while her father raged about the yard in a drunken fit, firing his pistol over their heads while the lightning split the darkness.

I know about the little African-American church near her home where she would hide from him. She spent a lot of time alone at that church. I think that's where she learned to pray. On Sunday morning she was a sad little white girl in a rolling sea of black faces. They loved her and let their little clapboard building be a refuge and a sanctuary. They are why her father could not destroy her faith in God.

He hurt her but could not drag her down. He twisted her, but she never snapped. For a time he owned her body, but never her soul.

He never apologized or admitted the great evil they all lived with. Neither did the rest of the family. So Chris left them. She left them all. She grew up, and she made good, in spite of what they said about her. She worked hard and made her own way in the world. She walked herself down the aisle and married one of the kindest, gentlest men I know.

She became very strong. As strong as a person can be who never had a daddy.

She stayed tender too. She has a very delicate and soft heart. That's where her poetry comes from. She writes from the back pew of that wooden church. She writes on the days when her legs won't reach the floor. She has managed to stay in touch with that lonely little girl. Thank God for tender mercies.

She is a little rough on the outside. She had to be. She's blunt, competitive, and a little suspicious. People misunderstand her at times, but if you will hold onto her and refuse to let go, she can lay a blessing on you for sure.

Last year she told our church family that God was leading her to pray for her fa-

ther. She admitted she didn't want to, and she assured us she wasn't going to seek contact with him. But she did make an agreement with God to pray. Even after all he did, she was willing to give him a smidgen of her sacred time in front of the little shrine she built in her home.

There was no miraculous change in him. That was not the point of her praying. He didn't change, and that wasn't a surprise.

I think the prayers were getting her ready for Monday.

When he died he took his final shot at her. Even as he breathed his last, he found a way to twist a knife in her old wound. She said it this way, "I never had a daddy, and now I know I never will."

She flinched, but did not bow her head. She did not curse his name. She gave him one last prayer and said, "Goodbye, Daddy."

And I tell you he will not be permitted to hurt her again.

She will be fine. She and her husband have a strong marriage. They share their faith in God together. They are good parents, and they have not passed his curse to their daughter.

The next time I see her, I'll walk straight up to her and give her a hug. I'll tell her what a blessing she is, and I'll let her know that a lot of people are thinking of her this week.

We are the very body of Christ in this gosh-awful world. To my way of thinking, that means when I hug Chris, it will be you hugging her as well.

And with all our arms around her, it will be Jesus holding her close, whispering that it's going to be okay.

The Preacher

Forgiveness

Forgiveness is the healing of wounds caused by another. You choose to let go of a past wrong and no longer be hurt by it. Forgiveness is a strong move to make, like turning your shoulders sideways to walk quickly on a crowded sidewalk.

It's your move.

It really doesn't matter if the person who hurt you deserves to be forgiven. Forgiveness is a gift you give yourself. You have things to do and you want to move on.

You can't forget. Forgiving has nothing to do with forgetting. You should remember everything and learn from it. Forgiving is goodness in the middle of remembering.

Above all, forgiveness is a series of choices you make.

You choose not to seek revenge or fantasize about revenge. You choose not to talk badly about the person who hurt you or wish evil for them.

You choose to let go of your anger and not to feed upon it. Shedding anger takes time and practice, but you choose to move in that direction.

You choose to wish that person well.

If these choices seem impossible to you, you might start by choosing to pray for the person who wronged you. You can pray for someone even if you don't believe in God.

You should be quiet about your forgiveness, except with close friends. If you need to tell the story, you have not arrived. Choose not to tell the story until you no longer want to.

Forgiveness does not always lead to a healed relationship. Some people are not capable of love, and it might be wise to let them go along with your anger. Wish them well, and let them go their way.

Whatever happens, forgiveness is good food for your soul.

The Preacher

This is what preaching should be

On **Monday** she selects the scripture for Sunday's sermon. She reads it. She prays. She thinks. She reads what others have said about the text. She doodles. She frets. She puts the Bible aside and goes about her business, but the passage is always on her mind. She becomes a watcher and a student of life. She is on the trail of new connections and new ways of seeing.

Tuesday is the day of pain and joy. She is sometimes broken by the passage and sometimes carried away to places unspoken. What is suggested by the text is beyond belief, like a madman's story. She is out of her mind with hope. She is a dreamer and a wisher and a punch-drunk pilgrim.

She would never claim to have an absolute handle on scripture, but on **Wednesday** she thinks she has heard the story.

On **Thursday** she begins searching for a way to tell this story. She wants the Bible to come alive for her friends the way it lives for her. She talks to herself a lot in the second half of the week. Her spouse has gotten used to this.

By **Friday** afternoon she must have her outline. The intro is huge. How will we begin this journey on Sunday? she wonders. The transitions must be smooth. She wants to tell one true thing and tell it well. She NEVER uses canned illustrations and cheap stories. God forbid.

On **Sunday** morning she arrives before the sun, stands in the pulpit and preaches to the darkness. When she is as ready as she will be, the work is done and the relief makes her giddy. She relaxes and peeps out the window to see if her friends have arrived. Not yet. Not yet. Not yet.

This is the preaching life. This is the life she has chosen and the life chosen for her. Don't ask her how both can be true. They just are.

The big moment comes, and she stands before her dear friends. She has not earned the right to speak, but she has been called to do so. She would NEVER presume to preach to others. Only those who have asked will hear her story.

Her little secret is that Richard Pryor taught her to preach, taught her to make them want to listen. She is funny but never tells jokes. She speaks first of her own journey with the Bible that very week. She is transparent just beyond the point of comfort, when people start to look away. Careful, not too transparent — watch those boundaries. She lives on the razor edge between preaching and sharing.

She never, ever goes too long.

When the sermon is over, she does not want to make eye contact, but she does. She is ashamed because she is proud when she moves them. She has never been able to conquer her pride.

On a good Sunday, she can see that her friends have engaged the Bible with her in an authentic way. What they do with this is out of her hands and perhaps none of her business.

For the first five years she believed she had done something very important when she delivered a good sermon. In year six she began to realize that sermons aren't so important in the scheme of things. That year she said publicly that the woman watching the children during the service was giving the greater gift.

In year eight she truly began to believe this.

She does everything possible to de-emphasize the sermon. She does not leave printed manuscripts in the foyer. She does not sell tapes. She does not post sermons on the church website. She is not strong enough to withstand that kind of temptation. Every sermon is a sand painting, created with all the energy she can muster and blown away on the winds of her voice.

They love each other, the woman and her people. They are in this together, for the long haul. Her best sermons are like the whispers of dear friends and lovers.

The Preacher

Kippy's story

Part 1: Recovering Kippy

A wave of child noise broke across our living room the other day. There was a warning rumble of feet and a crash of complaining followed by giggling breakers. A small part of me was paying attention — about 5 percent, I reckon.

Having small children is like living on a reef. Tides of energy roll in and out of rooms. Noises swell and recede. Your mind sways in the current, like a sea plant, and then settles back.

That's what I was doing on this day. Swaying with the waves and trying to stay anchored to my book. Hearing the noise, but not hearing it, if you know what I mean. I was doing a pretty good job of it too, until one word separated itself from the muted buzz, becoming louder and more clear. It definitely got my attention.

My youngest daughter said, "Kippy."

I experienced a jolt of emotion and was instantly on high alert. This word was familiar to me, but I couldn't remember anything about it. I could sense that there was a powerful memory lurking nearby. I was sniffing at the edges of something important.

I kept saying the word over and over, trying to coax the memory to the surface. "Kippy, Kippy, Kippy." I wanted this memory, but it was playing hard to get. The harder I concentrated, the more it eluded me.

Recovering a memory can be tricky. You have to sneak up on it. You have to give up, walk away, and see if it follows you. I slowed to a mental jog and was turning back to my book when a lovely image popped into my mind. I could see my oldest daughter, Reiley, twelve years ago when she was only two. She used to say "Kippy." It was one of her little words.

Properly primed, the memory rose and overflowed its levee, flooding me with the silt of 1991. It all came back.

That was the year Christy showed up. My wife Jeanene and I were young, with only one child. Christy was a sad and lonely woman who somehow found her way to our little church. Reiley called her "Kippy," and offered her the pure nectar of a child's love. Kippy hadn't had much love in her life, so she took a pull from that little mug and then stayed for seconds. She made herself a part of our family for a time.

Kippy, where are you now, I wonder?

Christy was a self-proclaimed victim of ritual abuse, a subject I learned a lot about during the time of our friendship. In the 1980s there was a flood of reported cases of ritualistic abuse by satanic cults. The victims of SRA, as it came to be called, reported thousands of rapes, ritual killings, and other crimes.

Many of these accusations came from "recovered memories" that were unearthed in therapy sessions. The whole thing played right into the hands of some Christian groups who have a need to believe in a worldwide satanic conspiracy.

That my own memory of Kippy had to be recovered is, well, interesting.

Law enforcement officials never found any evidence of organized ritual abuse, and the hype eventually subsided. Satanic ritual abuse had a lot in common with witch-hunts, hysteria, and urban legends. I'm not saying that no one was ever abused in a ritual setting. Anything and everything happens in isolated cases, but the SRA craze clearly got out of hand.

Christy found us at the end of a whirlwind tour of churches in our area. Her pattern was to show up at a church and tell shocking stories of ritual abuse at the hands of her own father. He was, according to her, the head of some secret satanic organization. She would hang around until her act wore thin and then move on.

Christy told me her stories, and I yawned. I heard her for a little while and then changed the subject. "Yeah, yeah, whaddya wanna do for lunch?" I don't have the energy it takes to talk about Satan. It bores me, and I have a very short attention span.

When I didn't react or call an emergency prayer meeting, Christy stopped telling the stories. After a few weeks she got a job, and eventually joined our church. She fell in love with Reiley and started hanging out at our house. It was okay because we liked her. We really did. She spent Christmas with us in 1991. We were too poor to travel, and she had nowhere to go.

After a while, Jeanene and I kinda forgot about the Satan stories. Christy seemed normal enough, and she became a close friend. We even let her baby-sit. I look back now and realize how crazy we were to take a chance like that. We were young and trying to be like Jesus, a dangerous combination.

I think we were all in denial.

The relationship lasted about nine months, as I recall, and then Christy left us. Our friendship came to an end in one shocking moment of relapse and betrayal.

Maybe she wanted to return to her world of demons and fear. Maybe she was getting bored playing Pictionary with us on Friday nights. Maybe she believed what she thought happened at our house that day.

I don't know what she thinks. I only know what happened.

Now that I think of it, being a pastor is also like living on a reef. You never know what the tide will bring. People come and go like waves, some carrying pain and some bringing nourishment. You bend and sway with the swells, but you must keep your roots firmly anchored. You can never let go of your rock. You live in the current, but not at its mercy.

You do not want to get washed out to sea.

Part 2: Kippy's betrayal

It all started when I found an old copy of *Faust* at a used bookstore.

The image on the cover of this book is the alchemical symbol for the "Principle of Mercury," whatever that is. What I know about alchemy can be written Henry David style, right on my thumbnail.

I'd never read *Faust*, but I thought I might like to someday. I bought the book and tossed it into the back seat of my car, where it sat for a couple of weeks.

Christy noticed the book when she was helping me unload some groceries. All of a sudden she shouted, "Oh my God," and shot out of the car.

"That's a satanic book," she said, pointing to the back seat. There was a wild, panicked look in her eyes.

I rushed over, alarmed by the tone of her voice. "What? What book?"

"That book in the car. That's a satanic symbol. I remember seeing it during one of my father's black masses. Oh my God!"

I had no idea what she was talking about, but she was creeping me out. I leaned into the car, looked around, and saw the book. I exhaled loudly, relieved. Damn, that girl spooked me.

I shouted from inside the car, "Hey, it's nothing. It's just my copy of *Faust*. Nothing to worry about."

I thought it was a simple misunderstanding. Given her history, it was understandable that the symbol on the cover might scare her. I figured we'd be laughing about this by supper.

I was wrong. I backed out of the car and found her in a hysterical state. She was looking around like she thought her daddy was going to jump out from behind a bush.

I didn't understand what was happening at the time, but I think I do now. Christy initially thought that someone from her father's cult had planted the book as a kind of creepy warning to her. She thought it was a message to let her know they knew where she was. Her stories were full of stuff like that. According to Christy, you could never leave a satanic group. They would use their dark powers to find you. They would never give up.

There was a kind of paranoid grandiosity to the whole thing. Christy was center stage, her soul of the highest value to the forces of evil. They would stop at nothing to find her. It was very Jungian, the dark side of Christianity surfacing in a bad dream.

At the time I just wanted to calm her down. I tried to tell her the truth about the book. "Whoa, slow down. It's okay. Listen, it's not a satanic book; it's just *Faust.*

"What's Faust?"

"It's an old story — a classic. It's about a guy who . . . well, it's just this old story, you know, about a guy who, uh, has, um, some troubles. It's German; it's this German story."

I admit I wasn't making a whole lot of sense. I was talking and trying to figure out what was going on in Christy's head. As I talked I was also realizing that I probably shouldn't go into any details about Faust selling his soul to Mephistopheles.

For a second I thought she was calming down. She seemed to hear me. She stopped breathing so hard, and she looked right at me. I smiled, thinking the whole episode was over.

It was the last time we would ever make eye contact.

"It's YOUR book?"

I mistook the tone in her voice for relief. "Sure," I said, still not anticipating what was to come.

She stared at me for a few seconds, and then I saw something I hope I never see again. I watched her feelings for me turn from love to hatred in a matter of seconds. I saw the whole transformation in her face. It began with a blank look of bewilderment, then her eyes narrowed with suspicion. She shook her head a few times in denial, as though she didn't want to believe the worst. Finally her jaw set and anger flashed in her eyes.

It was like watching one of those horror movies where a spell is broken, and the corpse goes from flesh to dust in five seconds.

"You're one of them," she said, backing away.

I was stunned to the point of losing speech. My feet were glued to the ground. I managed a weak protest.

"What? No! Christy! Are you kidding me? I never . . ."

I don't think she heard me. She was already moving for her car. She jumped in and started the engine. I ran toward her, but her tires were already squealing on the pavement. She was gone.

In the years since, I have developed a pretty thick skin. That's a paradox of ministry. You have to have a thick and a thin skin. You have to learn to hold compassion and detachment in balance. It takes years to learn this art.

I was much younger then, and all I had was the thin skin I was born with. What she said wasn't true, but it was horribly painful to know that someone thought I was evil and involved in a conspiracy of abuse. I felt bad inside, almost like it WAS true. I felt real bad. I couldn't shake it, either. Not for a couple of weeks.

Every time I heard Reiley's little voice say, "Where's Kippy?" my heart would crack open again.

Christy left a bunch of her stuff in our guest room, so I thought we might see her again. I hoped she would come to her senses. When the doorbell rang a few days later, I thought it might be her.

It wasn't. Instead, two very serious looking women were on my front porch. They looked at me with pure hatred in their eyes.

"We're here for Christy's things," they said, pushing past me into the house.

One of them hastily scooped Christy's stuff into a cardboard box. The other one never took her eyes off me. She watched me closely, like I might put a hex on them. I noticed her lips were moving as she whispered constant prayers for protection.

I was their worst nightmare, a worshipper of Satan posing as a preacher, leading a whole congregation to hell. A vicious traitor, a thief of souls.

Christy had told me about a radical group of Christians that served as a kind of witness relocation program for people who had escaped ritual abuse. I assumed these women were a part of that group.

When they finished gathering her things, they left without a word. As they drove away I could see Christy in the back seat, her head bowed.

She did not turn around and look back.

For the record, I have no idea how much of Christy's story was true, if any. I suspect she did have an abusive father. In some parts of the Christian world, adding a satanic spin to your story can get you a lot of sympathy. Bodyguards even. I think she needed the attention and slipped the story on like a familiar jacket. Memories can be tricky to manage, especially when you are dredging them out of your pain.

That *Faust* is the book that caused all this is, well, interesting. I never did read it, but I keep the book on my shelf as a reminder of . . . something. I don't know what. It has survived several book purges over the years as I've moved toward simplicity. For some reason, I can never bring myself to get rid of it.

I have no idea where Christy is today, but I'm guessing she tells this story too. Perhaps she gathers the faithful around her and tells of the day she almost got dragged back into Satanism by the counterfeit preacher. Thank God she spotted the book in time. The Lord always provides a way for the faithful.

We share a common story, separated by radically different memories. Recovered memories, perhaps. Our stories follow very different paths, but they both end in the same place.

Betrayal.

The Preacher

Fundamentalism hurts

Fundamentalism makes for interesting television, doesn't it? Hearing Jerry Falwell say that abortionists, pagans, and feminists (among others) caused the 9-11 disaster was nauseofascinating. Watching a man hold a sign that says, "God hates fags" is like watching film clips of the holocaust. Can such things be?

Oh, they be.

If you want to know about the Taliban, ask an Afghani woman. If you want to know about Christian fundamentalism, ask a Christian. Fundamentalists are more than interesting television for us. They are people with real power who harm our churches, destroy good ministers, and sully our name.

We've been in the cages with these cats, and they go for the jugular. They are always on the prowl, circling the campfires of the followers of Christ, howling the name of Jesus and splattering our heritage across their banners of hatred.

Watching fundamentalism do its work is like watching the crucifixion over and over and over again.

Never confuse fundamentalism with a particular set of beliefs. Fundamentalism is a methodology. It is a way of relating to people. There are fundamentalist Christians, fundamentalist Muslims, and don't forget the politically correct zealots. You will meet fundamentalists in every walk of life.

Fundamentalism's method is confrontation and its fuel is anger. There can be no dialogue and no mutual respect. There will only be winners and losers. They are right. You are wrong. End of discussion.

Fundamentalist Christians also carry a terrible, secret burden. Your soul is their responsibility. If you go to hell, they will answer to God for their lack of witness. Imagine carrying THAT load around all day. Naive Christians are shackled to this burden by pastors whose need to enlarge their personal church kingdom has an "Enron" feel to it.

With such hellish stakes, extreme measures are called for. The end justifies the means. This is why so many Christian fundamentalists want to use the government to push their agenda.

Ultimately fundamentalists will consume their own young and gnaw at their own flesh. The way of anger always leads to consumption.

But the way of anger was never supposed to be our way.

Did you know we were first called Christians in Antioch of Syria? Before that, the followers of Jesus simply called themselves, "People of The Way." They believed they were called to follow the way of Christ.

You cannot follow the way of Christ and walk in the way of anger. You just cannot.

The way of Christ is for those with nothing to prove and nothing left to lose. It is not anger and conquest that sustains you on "The Way."

What sustains you is the simple placing of one foot in front of the other, all The Way to the end.

The Preacher

I pledge allegiance to the blue shoes girl

I pledged allegiance to a little girl in blue shoes yesterday. We all did. The crossing guard shot off the curb with her whistle in her mouth and her white gloves and her specious authority. All the cars stopped for one little girl with blue shoes who was a little late for school.

She had no idea that all the cars were waiting on her. She stepped off the curb with exaggerated caution, like she was sticking a toe in cold water. Halfway across, something on the ground caught her eye, and she bent over to look at it. The crossing guard had to beep her whistle and give her a head jerk to keep her moving.

And then I swear she used three different walks to get to the other side. There was a skippy little pony-walk, a bunny-hop or two, and finally some kind of slap-happy thing that I'm pretty sure is from a Bugs Bunny cartoon.

There was a flash of blue and a backpack slapping on a tiny bottom, and then she was gone.

Little blue shoes girl, you do not know who you are, but we know, and we are struck dumb. We can only stare through the parted waters as you dance your way across the Jordan.

Did you know we have a law for you? We made a law so that on our worst days we would not forget. Even on the days when we think being at work on time is more important than little girls in blue shoes, a woman with gloves and a whistle will stop us and make us remember who you are.

Some of us say there is something eternal about you, something we call a soul. We don't exactly know what we mean by that; it might be our way of saying you are eleventy-hundred infinity good. But if there is anything eternal in you, any scent of the creator lying soft on the back of your neck, then you are worth more than all the gold and all the mountains and all the world.

Some of us do not believe in souls and do not like to throw words like "eternal" around carelessly, but we can't deny that you are the most amazing thing we have ever seen. In all our searching and in throwing the best we have at looking deep and far, you pausing in the street to examine whatever it was that interested you is the rarest mystery of all. We've only seen this once, and it's right here at home, right here in your little heart.

No one knows what you will be when you grow up. You may be a force for good in this world, or you may bring great evil upon us. You have that power. You have those choices, and this is why we stop and stare.

But whatever you do, or whatever is done to you, on November 13, 2003, you were the little girl with blue shoes who carried unthinkable goodness across the street.

No one is able to take that away from you.

The Preacher

Little black book

At the macro and micro levels, the universe presents as a smooth, impenetrable mystery. Without instruments, the sky is an innocent dome and the world in every grain of sand remains safely hidden from view.

Instruments give us purchase. Scientists run their hands along the casing of reality, looking for leverage points. When they find one, they wiggle an instrument in there and lean on it good. The carapace pops, and there is a whoosh of escaping air. Cautiously they peer inside, looking for the inevitable surprises.

I read that the scientists who jimmied the DNA box spooked a gaggle of wild RNA strands that scattered and ran giggling around the lab. These little delinquents refuse to make proteins like good RNAs should. What they like to do is meddle in the complex process of gene suppression.

They call them "Interfering RNAs."

Beautiful.

It sounds more like a daycare center than a lab.

I can picture the lead scientist barking commands. *"Stedman, round up every last one of those interfering little bastards, and find out what the hell they're up to."*

The universe. You gotta love her. Look up or down, she can't be found. She doesn't like to give up her secrets. She's seductive, sliding her lace along her legs. She's a shameless flirt, winking in the night sky, getting the scientists all worked up.

A word of warning: you won't even get to second base with this girl. She's got the ultimate chaperone — the speed of light.

FYI, I hear the speed of light has a Scottish brogue.

"I dinnae care how big your telescope is, laddie. Put it back in your trousers. You can look nae further."

Some things are forever beyond our vision. We cannot see the present moment, for example. We have to wait on light, and the time lag gets downright inconvenient when looking across the galaxy.

Does anyone really believe that we will discover a unified theory? Doesn't that seem wildly hopeful, like high school boys trying to take off a bra?

A wonderful myth in Genesis tells the story of when the first humans were cast out of the Garden of Eden. God set cherubim and a flaming sword east of Eden, guarding the way to the tree of life.

Forget those modern pictures of little baby angels. Cherubim will flat kick your ass, with or without flaming swords. They don't have Scottish accents, but they make themselves understood.

You can go no further.

There's a reason the Bible is a little black book. It's not pornography. It doesn't rip the dress off lady creation and lay bare her secrets for panting adolescents.

This little black book is for people who want to play the seductive and secretive game of spirituality. It's full of hints and tricks that sometimes work, but not always. There are phone numbers you can try on a lonely night. There are stories of people who were close to Truth, close enough to see the hem of her garment. Close enough to catch the glow of her face.

The Bible presents reality not as a smooth casing to be leveraged and popped open. The Bible presents reality as intimacy — as God incarnate.

Mystery.

Slip your finger under the strap and gently slide it off her shoulder. Check the little black book for a good opening line, and see how far you get with her tonight. Feel the warmth of this flesh. Moisten your lips for a kiss. This is the reality you have always longed for. This is the consummation of your deepest need. This is prayer.

Turn your head in the darkness and whisper your desire.

"Are you there? Do you love me?"

The Preacher

Toward a theology of feet

"I'm serious," he said. "Give me your foot."

They were on the ugly, yellow loveseat that his in-laws had given them. It was in the master bedroom so the kids would have somewhere to sleep if they got scared at night.

His daughter was lying on her back with her head propped on a pillow and her feet in his lap. She lifted one foot, and he held it with his right hand. He raised his left thumb and put it next to her foot.

"You remember I told you that when you were born your foot was only as big as my thumb?"

"Yes."

"Well, look. See how much bigger your foot is now that you're six? There's a lot more *foot stuff* here, see?" He lightly pinched all over her foot. "Where do you think all that *stuff* comes from? Where do you think your body gets all the *stuff* it needs to make your feet bigger?"

"I don't know," she said, looking right into his eyes. She was hooked, and he loved having her mind all to himself. His fourteen-year-old turned away from the computer to listen. She was hooked too, and it was like finding a second fish on the line.

"The stuff your feet are made of comes from food. We can't create or destroy matter. The only thing we can do is rearrange it. We have this handy little hole in front, see. You shove apples or bread or beans in there, and your body turns that food into feet."

"Even Skittles?" the little one asked.

He winced and stroked his chin. "Well . . . yeah, but better foods make for better feet."

The older daughter broke in, "Da-ad!" She made two syllables out of the word, changing pitch to show her skepticism.

His expression didn't change and she lost her confidence. "You swear?"

"I promise. Look, plants are machines that turn dirt into fruits and vegetables. We are machines that turn fruits and vegetables and other stuff into feet."

They were silent, both mouths hanging open. He let the pause hang in the air before his coup d'état.

"So really, if you think about it, we're all made of dirt."

An idea snapped the older one out of her slouch. "Hey, that's what the Bible says. It says God made humans out of dirt."

The little one nodded enthusiastically. She'd been to Sunday School. She'd heard that story.

"That's right," he said. "For an old book, the Bible can be pretty insightful at times."

The little one was staring off into space. He could tell her mind was racing a hundred miles an hour.

"You go, girl," he whispered as he slipped out of the room.

The Preacher

John the Baptist

I bought a blue jean priest shirt in a religious store. I'd never seen one made of denim. I don't normally wear a collar, but I AM ordained. I can wear one if I want.

I think I'll wear it to play disc golf. I'll wear it with my ratty shorts, old sneakers, and wide-brimmed hat.

And with black socks.

Here's my fantasy about what will happen on that day:

I hit the first hole and a bunch of typical GenX slackers are waiting around to tee off. My outfit stuns them into silence. I'm either a grunge priest or the most blasphemous guy they've ever seen. I like it that they aren't sure which of these is true.

I speak first.

"You waitin' for someone?"

"Yeah."

"Mind if I go ahead and play through?"

"Sure."

I drop my disc bag and unzip it. They catch the flash of color and understand that I have serious plastic. All high quality. All fly-dye. You don't carry discs like this unless you know what you're doing.

I pull out a handful of paperback New Testaments and pass them around. I'm one short. I hesitate a second, then pull a beer out of my disc bag and give that to the last guy.

"Sorry dude, I'm out of Bibles."

They receive these gifts like some people receive communion — with childlike stares. It seems like something important is happening, but they aren't exactly sure what it is.

I put my hand up like a gospel singer to feel the air. The breeze is with me and slightly right, so I pull out my 170-gram Cheetah, the one with the very cool dye job. I roll my head around and work my wrist a couple of times before yankin that sumbitch down the fairway, right-center. My snap is enough to turn it over a bit, so it yawns right before fading left and parking right at the base of the basket.

"Booyah."

While I'm gathering up my shit I can hear the silence behind me. I turn around and give em the good word.

"That's the power of prayer, my sons. The power of prayer. Now turn from your wicked-ass ways."

I'm halfway down the fairway before they close their mouths.

I have the blue jean priest shirt.

I play the game.

I own the cool discs and the Bibles.

My theology is plenty earthy.

If the good Lord will grant me a great tee shot, this thing could absolutely happen.

Matthew 3:1-10

www.pdga.com

The Preacher

David's two-by-four

I spent the whole morning yesterday on the roof of the new building our church is constructing. It's a "little cottage in the woods" kind of thing.

Of course, the question you may be asking is "What the hell were you doing on the roof?"

It's a fair question and one my wife has been asking me since she heard about my close call.

You might remember David Kramer from the Elliot stories. Jennifer and David Kramer almost ran out of our church the night their son bit Elliot, but Carol nailed herself into the road and wouldn't let them pass.

The Kramers still attend our church, though sporadically. Their marriage has been "on-again off-again." They've had some close calls, but someone has always been there to keep them from going over the edge. Someone always helps them see a reason to keep trying.

David is a roofer with very rough hands and rougher ways. He spends his days working alone in the brutal South Texas sun. He's a hard worker and a hard man, but he's got a soft heart, almost like a baby's heart, I'd say.

When I heard that David wanted to put the roof on the new building, I impulsively volunteered to help him. Our construction manager, who is also a church member, looked over the top of his glasses at me with a dubious smile.

Anyway, that's how I came to be on the roof of a very tall building yesterday. We have a 9-pitch roof, which is quite steep. If you fall you drop eighteen feet onto jagged piles of the limestone we're using for the exterior walls.

Welcome to David Kramer's world.

David scampered about like a mountain goat, but I scrabbled around on all fours like a crab, clinging to anything that would keep me from sliding off. Here and there David nailed two-by-fours down for purchase. These became little oases of safety for me. I would crab-walk my way to one of these boards and hate it when I had to move on.

For two hours I crawled around trying to help but too frightened to stand up. I was very awkward, like the people who go down ladders facing out. David was talking to me the whole time, spouting esoteric roofing wisdom in short Confucian bursts.

"Respect the roof, but don't fear the roof. Fearin' it can get you killed."

At one point he commanded me with Christ-like authority, saying, "Don't be afraid. Stand up and walk."

I stood and I did walk. I did walk on a 9-pitch roof, and I felt proud.

During a water break, we got to talk a little. He said, "You remember the night Jr. bit Elliot all up?"

"Yeah, I remember."

"Well, he's doin' better now since we been at church. He ain't bit no kids. Plays with 'em better too. We 'preciate the help this church has done."

He was trying to tell me something, but I was too preoccupied with my fear to hear him.

And then I stepped on a patch of sawdust and fell. My feet shot out behind me, dumping me on my knees and my face. I rolled onto my back as I slid, my heels ripping a swath through the tarpaper as I frantically tried to dig in.

David's voice called out without panic, "Catch hold-a that two-by-four."

Sliding on my bottom, I was stopped near the edge of the roof by the board he had anchored with his strong hands. Bleeding and disheveled, I looked up at David, but he was already back to work.

At that moment I understood that David's work was his way of saying thanks. Some dear people nailed themselves to the deck when David and Jennifer were going over the edge. He was just returning the favor in his own way.

With my feet on that two-by-four and my heart pounding, I laid my head back on the roof to catch my breath.

David, I think we're all even.

The Preacher

I have no title for this

Sit down, Christian. You cannot wave your unread Bible and scare me because I know the larger story that runs through it from beginning to end. I'm trying to resist the temptation to snatch if from your hands and beat you with it. I am your worst nightmare, a Texas preacher who knows the good book better than you do. Show me your scriptures. Show me how you justify condemning homosexual people.

Show me what you got, Christian. The Sodom story? That story is about people who wanted to commit a brutal rape. Let's all say it together, "God doesn't like rape." You could have listened to your heart and learned that, Christian. Move on. What else you got?

A passage from Leviticus? Are you kidding me? Are you prepared to adhere to the whole Levitical code of behavior? No? Then why would you expect others to? Move on. What else?

Two passages — two verses from Romans and one from 1 Corinthians. There you stand, your justification for a worldwide campaign of hatred written on two limp pieces of paper. Have you looked closely at these passages? Do you understand their context and original language? I could show you why you don't have much, but there is something more important you need to see.

Come with me to the church cellar. Come now and don't delay. I am shaking with anger and fighting the urge to grab you by the collar and drag you down these steps.

You didn't know the church had a cellar? Oh yes, every church does. Down, down we go into the darkness. Don't slip on the flagstone and never mind the heat.

There, do you see the iron furnace door, gaping open? Do you see the roaring flames? Do you see the huge man with glistening muscles, covered with soot? Do you see him feeding the fire with his massive, scooped shovel?

He feeds these flames with the Bible, with every book, chapter, and verse that American Christians must ignore to support our bloated lifestyles, our selfishness, our materialism, our love of power, our neglect of the poor, our support of injustice, our nationalism, and our pride.

See how frantically he works? Time is short, and he has much to burn. The prophets, the Shema, whole sections of Matthew, most of Luke, the entire book of James. Your blessed ten commandments? Why would you want to post them on courtroom walls when you've burned them in your own cellar?

Do you see? DO YOU SEE? Do you see how we rip, tear, and burn scripture to justify our lives?

The heat from this cursed furnace rises up and warms the complacent worshippers in the pews above. The soot from the fire blackens our stained glass so that we may not see out and no one wants to see in.

Do you smell the reek of this injustice? It is a stink in the nostrils of the very living God. We are dressed in beautiful clothes and we wear pretty smiles, but we stink of this blasphemous hypocrisy.

Every church in America — mine not excepted — has a cellar like this. We must shovel 24 hours a day, 7 days a week, 365 days a year, because every chapter and verse we ignore must be burned to warm our comfy pews.

Our souls are stained from this biblical holocaust, but somehow these two scraps of scripture mean all the world to you. You swallow whole camels, and now you're gagging on a gnat? When did you ever give a shit about what the Bible has to say?

Sit down, Christian. Sit down and be you silent.

How long has it been since you forgot that we were called to walk the earth as pilgrims? Do you not remember when he told us to give our coats to those in need and sell our possessions to help the poor? Did you forget how the first church had all things in common so that none would lack?

Did you forget the day he told us that whatever we did for the oppressed we did for him, and whatever we withheld from them was kept from him as well?

Sit down, Christian. You have not earned the right to speak to this generation. The right to speak is earned with love.

Take back your Bible. Take it back and start reading it. Fall in love again with Jesus. Sell what you must and walk the earth. Let your love be astonishing and people may one day listen to your words.

Even now you might be saved. Our God is merciful and forgiveness awaits.

The Preacher

TV preachers

I saw a TV preacher the other day. I was flipping through the channels, like men do, and there he was. A haircut with a floppy Bible and a Plexiglas pulpit. He was pacing the stage like a rapper, arms moving and talking a hundred miles an hour.

TV preachers fascinate me to no end. They have so much emotional energy. It's tiring just watching them.

I wonder if they pay high interest on their emotional debt, like I do. The body is a loan shark. You WILL pay premium rates to pull that kind of intensity at the time and place of your choosing. You will pay or lose a pound of flesh. This is something I know about.

Of course, if they're faking, they've made other arrangements. There are black market bargains to be had. Dark covenants can be cut, but let us not speak of such things.

This particular TV preacher could flat do it, too. He had that intangible thing that people have who can connect with audiences. Stand-up comedians have it, the good ones anyway. Motivational speakers have it. The guys in infomercials have it. Clinton had it. Bush doesn't.

I know what "it" is, and "it" is dangerous as hell, let me tell you.

So I watched this guy for a few minutes. I was amazed at the number of religious catch phrases, buzz words, and spiritual slogans he could pack between two breaths. There was no way my mind could keep up with his mouth.

It was like hearing George Carlin recite his long list of dirty words. You can't keep up. By the time you're done laughing at one, he's rattled off six more. Eventually you just give up and fall back on a rolling bed of laughter. You drink in the cadence of his voice. You hold what you can and let the rest go. You give yourself to Carlin, letting him keep up with where you've been and where you're going.

That's what it's like with these fast-talking TV preacher types. You either turn them off or give them something you know you should keep for yourself.

I listened for awhile with my mouth open. At some point I became aware that I was moving my face in slow circles. Counter-clockwise, I'm sure of it. Clockwise doesn't feel right.

According to the ancients, you should never leave your mouth wide open. My bad, I guess, and there was no one to say gesundheit either. An evil spirit must have hit the moving target because my soul started to feel bad. I've gone over it a hundred times in my mind, and that's the best way to say it. My soul felt bad. Real bad. It was like depression, but with a dash of Tabasco panic. A panicky tang to heighten a very dark mood.

And then I heard that voice that sometimes comes to me. I only listened for a moment before I slammed my mind shut to him. But he got his shot in.

"What are you looking at, asshole? That's you. He's a preacher. You're a preacher. I mean, he's better at it than you, but you're the same animal. Take a look in the mirror, preacher. Like what you see? You're a jack-booted, lock-step, weak-minded Jesus Nazi. You hack. You pimp. You pusher. You can soften the message, pretty it up like you do, make it sound more sophisticated, but . . ."

I spoke a powerful word against the voice. I said, "NO!" And I turned off the TV while I was at it. I have learned not to listen to that voice. I have also learned that it takes a couple of hours for the depression to fade. That's okay. I stopped being in a hurry some years back.

But this is the truth: Whenever I see a TV preacher, I cannot believe that I'm a preacher too. I cannot believe those guys are colleagues.

Stop right there. I know what you're going to say, and I don't want you to say it.

Do not tell me that I'm different. Do not tell me that TV preachers are con artists, but I'm not like them. Do not tell me that.

Yellow freakin' fear is the only thing keeping me safe. It just might save my soul, if my soul can be saved. Even as I write this I wonder if anyone can preach and be saved. Check that. No one can preach and be saved. Can't happen.

Of course, what's impossible for me, might still be possible for God. So God is my only hope and refuge. A very present help in times of trouble.

Be afraid, preachers. Be very afraid. Never forget what you could become, may yet become, may have become.

I cannot tell you how I know this, but I KNOW that I must not distance myself from the TV preachers. I must claim the same calling and run scared for the rest of my life.

I must open my mouth wide and force their reputation down my gullet, swallowing hard, then snapping my teeth like Val Kilmer did in "Top Gun."

If I meet someone who asks what I do, I must say, "preacher," and nothing else. I must stand quietly and make eye contact. I must never say, "But I'm not like those TV preachers."

It has to be this way. My life will tell my story, or my story will not be told. No words allowed, preacher. You're too good with words, and you know it.

I am a preacher. For twenty minutes a week, I preach. When I finish preaching I sit down and am ashamed. But I am willing, for someone must proclaim the day of the Lord.

The Preacher

Goodbye, Iron Giant

Saturday before last, I found a little boy under my table eating M&Ms. He was clearly eyeing my Iron Giant action figure.

"Go ahead, you can play with it," I said.

He grabbed it and ran down the hall. I stepped to the door to watch him go and felt an M&M crunch under my shoe.

Saturday night is when the charismatic Christians use our church building. I call them flower children. Sometimes I drop by and alternate between working in my office and listening to their music.

This particular Saturday I came because their pastor dropped dead two days before.

His name was Eddie, and he had the brightest eyes of anyone I ever knew. They were so bright and engaging that you noticed it even in the newspaper obituary photo. Eddie and I were friends ever since that day he walked into our church and asked if they could use the building on Saturday nights. That was the first time I saw his eyes.

The last time was five days before he died, when he told me about the land they bought and the building they were planning. His eyes were on fire. He was so happy, and he was doing exactly what he thought he should do with his life.

Eddie wasn't like me. He had no mixed feelings about preaching. None. And he preached with power to a people who have no second thoughts. They raise their hands to heaven whenever they sing. Sometimes I would listen and think, "How can you be so sure of yourselves?" Sometimes I would sit in the back and wonder how I could get me some of that.

He died preaching, too. He was preaching in another town when the aneurism that was hiding in his brain ended his life. He was fifty.

The flower children were in shock, but decided to go on with their worship service that weekend. They felt Pastor Eddie would have wanted it that way. I decided to go and stand with them in their grief.

When they started singing, signs of sadness melted away. A hand or two were raised, then more and more until the whole room was filled with people reaching for God. Their voices grew stronger until the air was full of their singing. Watching those hands reaching upward brought me to tears.

After the service, I hugged a few flower children and shook some hands. Then I headed back to my office to get away from everyone.

That's when I found the little boy under my table eating M&Ms. He was a little flower child boy. I think he was about four. He looked a little guilty, and I could tell he thought he wasn't supposed to go in my office. I think the Iron Giant lured him in.

Of all the toys in my office, the Iron Giant was my favorite. He stands 22 inches high, talks, and eats metal cars. You can see how tempting that would be for a little boy. Sometimes I open the door and say, "Hey, Giant."

So I stepped on the M&M and watched him run down the hall with the Iron Giant under his arm, bumping against his little legs. His mother caught him and said, "No. You're not supposed to play with that." Then she saw me and said, "I'm sorry. He knows he's not supposed to go in your office, but he's always looking at that robot."

His older brother walked up and said, "Cool! The Iron Giant. I love that movie."

I walked down the hall toward them.

"It's okay. In fact, I want him to keep it. He can have it."

"Oh no," she said. "We can't . . ."

"No, really. Listen. I mean, like two weeks ago, I was thinking that the next little boy who came to my office and liked the Iron Giant could keep him. I was just waiting for that little boy to come along, and I guess tonight is the night."

I regretted it immediately, but I said it, and that's that. His mother thanked me more than she should have, and they walked away. The little boy was hugging the Iron Giant, and I think he kissed it. I can't be sure, but I think he did.

I didn't ask his name. He was a little flower child boy, and that's all I know. All the big people were sad, and he got the Iron Giant. That's all he knew about that night.

So I don't have the Iron Giant anymore. He's gone, and my office seems empty without him.

The Iron Giant was like a lot of good people I know. Strong, interesting, and out of place in this world. And with very shiny eyes. First you wonder where they came from, and later you wonder where they went, because they never stay as long as you would like.

They seem to have other things to do, good people. They take their shiny eyes, and they go away, and though you feel selfish about them, you just have to let them go. You have to. There is no other way.

The only comfort comes in thinking about how nice it was to know them, and how nice it was to brush against goodness for a season.

So, goodbye, Eddie.

Goodbye, Giant.

The Preacher

Superball spirituality

Things have been unpredictable around here. Eddie died, my friend Tom called to tell me his life is falling apart, and I found a Superball at church. It has a chunk gouged out of it so it bounces funny.

They do say these things come in threes.

Perhaps I should explain about Tom. He's a Baptist pastor in a town near mine. His wife came home recently and told him she wanted a divorce. They have three children, and he has to leave the house. He lost his family and his home in just a few hours.

It gets worse. Most Baptist churches do not want a divorced person to be their pastor. Pastors can be greedy, manipulating sons-of-bitches, but they better not be divorced. It's hypocritical and stupid, but that's the way it is.

I grew up Baptist, so I feel entitled to speak my mind here.

I met with Tom and his deacons the night he told them his family was falling apart. They were gentle and sympathetic. They told him he could stay on as pastor. They laid hands on him and prayed for him. They promised in Jesus' name they would stand behind him and walk with him through these hard days. He burst into tears because it was the first moment of grace he had received since the whole thing started.

That was Thursday night. Sunday morning they fired him, the chicken-shit bastards. They lied. Maybe they wanted to be nice and polite in front of the visiting pastor. So they prayed to Jesus while they made plans to toss Tom out like trash.

So now Tom is jobless and homeless. And I promise you Baptist churches aren't lining up to hire a divorced pastor who was fired from his last church. After eight years of education and ten years of service, he'll have to find some other way to live.

I'm so damn mad the only thing I can do is change the subject rather abruptly and tell you about the Superball I found at church.

Kids left it, I guess. I found it under the communion table. Eddie was dead and Tom was screwed, so I threw it as hard as I could against the wall and watched it bounce around the church.

However it sounds now, it made sense to me at the time.

A wall, a beam, a "bud-ah-bump" under a chair, a bad hop on the grout, and so on. It finally came to rest on a tile by the back door. I walked over to it and considered the unlikely series of events that brought the ball and me to this spot.

I had to say something.

"Behold. Of all the tiles in the room, you were chosen."

My second throw took a weird bounce off a music stand and damn near broke the communion chalice that Francis gave to the church in memory of her mother. I had a vague sense that this wasn't the sort of thing responsible pastors do in church. I am called to be something of a caretaker around here.

So I took the chalice down from the fireplace mantle and put it in the kitchen where it would be safe. Then I ran back to the sanctuary to play with my Superball some more.

I found that even if I threw it at the same spot on the wall, it never ended up in the same place on the floor. What with the irregular surfaces in the room and the chunk missing from the ball, there was no way to predict where it was going to end up.

Chaos. Our ancient foe.

Genesis says God hovered over the waters and brought order out of chaos with mighty words. I don't know about you, but that impresses the hell out of me. When you bring order out of chaos, you've done a day's work.

And since God went to all that trouble, lots of people come to church hoping to find an easy way out of chaos. They want to know the future or make sense of the past. They hope that preachers like me will speak a mighty word and bring order out of the mess.

I got news for you. I ain't God. I'm just a guy with a bad haircut bouncing a ball around the sanctuary and talking to himself.

Welcome to our church.

There are a lot of irregular surfaces here. Pews and tables and pulpits and that kind of stuff. And most of the people are wounded in one way or another. You take a guy with a chunk missing and bounce him off a communion table, and he's liable to end up just about anywhere.

That's half the fun.

People come through the doors broken and hopeless and end up teaching Sunday School. I've seen it. Other people arrive with all the answers and end up crying on the floor.

I mean, you just never know with church.

Tom said he wants to come to our church on Sunday. A big chunk has been taken out of his life, so he should feel right at home with us sinners. When he walks through the door he'll meet Evangelina and Pepe. He'll see Stan, Carol, and Elliot. God help him if Chloe gets to him first.

I haven't told you about Chloe. I'll have to do that one of these days.

And even though Tom's life seems like chaos right now, he'll be welcome to bounce around these walls with us as long as he likes. And who knows? One good bounce off the communion table could make all the difference.

The Superball? I took it to my office and gave it a place of honor right in Tigger's lap. I might take it down now and then and toss it around. Sometimes I need a little reminder of what church really is.

When life seems chaotic, you don't need people giving you easy answers or cheap promises. There might not be any answers to your problems. What you need is a safe place where you can bounce with people who have taken some bad hops of their own.

You need love and understanding and lots of room.

That's what church should be.

The Preacher

An open letter from a pastor to his new congregation

Before we begin this relationship, tell me the truth.

What do you want from me?

Do you want me timid and wearing little spectacles, droning from a dusty prayer book while people nod in the pews? Do you want a gentle eunuch, tamed and kept by the church gentry? Do you want to pull my chain and watch the pretty Jesus words come out?

Perhaps you want a mime. Maybe you want a preacher in stripes and suspenders with white gloves and nothing much to say. A guy with a perpetual smile, twisting balloon bunnies and handing out theological la-dee-das to the smiling crowds. Is that what you want?

What if I threw a Bible at you? Would you like that? What if I glared down at you from the pulpit and hurled a huge King James into the shrieking crowd? You want me to hurt you? You want me to tell you that you've been a bad doggie?

How about parlor tricks? A little sleight-of-hand and a candle behind the sheet. Is that what you're looking for? An empty wheelchair rolling down the aisle and a palm pressed against a forehead while I lean in close and whisper, "Lie down now, my child, for the cameras are rolling."

What if I walked into your church and fully half the congregants mouthed, "Oh shit"? What if I was wild and woolly, unshaven and with a scary look in my eyes? What if I had a Bible in one hand and a beer in the other? What if my breath stank of grasshoppers and my chin dripped honey? What if children ran to their parents and said they saw the preacher behind the church, cussing and eating dirt?

Do you want a crazy man in your pulpit?

And what if I was all of these things and none of these things? What

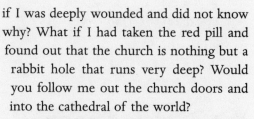

if I was deeply wounded and did not know why? What if I had taken the red pill and found out that the church is nothing but a rabbit hole that runs very deep? Would you follow me out the church doors and into the cathedral of the world?

What if all I could do was limp after the Gentle Shepherd along a very narrow and dangerous way? Would you follow me down that path? If I stopped and waited for you to walk beside me, would you?

And what if I tilted my head toward you until our foreheads touched and whispered the big secret?

There is no such thing in all the world as a preacher.

If I said that, would you laugh and walk with me arm-in-arm, all the way to the Promised Land?

The Preacher

Hollowed be thy name

These people asked me to do a wedding in a hollow church. I shit you not. A hollow church.

They found this place in Dallas. The congregation lost touch with their neighborhood and went away, leaving their building behind. I guess they went away; they're not there now. Maybe churches are like hermit crabs. When they want a new shell they just crawl away and leave the old one to whoever finds it.

Anyway, someone bought the building, gutted it, and turned it into an art gallery. The outside still looks like a cute little church, but inside there's nothing but walls going every which way, track lighting, and European bottled water arranged on tables.

They do a heckuva wedding business there, too. It's perfect for people who want the charm of a pretty church but are a little uncomfortable with what goes on inside churches.

So these people, the ones I was telling you about, they rented the hollow church and were looking for a minister to do the wedding.

They hoped to capture the classic beauty of the Christian ceremony without the bother of Christianity. They wanted the delicious English from the Book of Common Prayer, but they didn't want the Word behind the words, if you take my meaning. They were looking for someone to roll out our tradition, like a precious Torah scroll, so they could see it naked and lay familiar hands on it. They wanted to stretch it and pull it and slide it around on the table. They wanted to cut it into swatches and see if it matched the bridesmaids' dresses.

They needed a preacher in a robe who would deliver the goods with a wink and a smile, then go away and not bother anyone. They wanted someone they could call onstage and then dismiss with a wave and a little cash in an envelope.

They actually said to me, "We want a nice wedding and all. You know, classic. But can you tone down the God and Jesus stuff? We'll pay you, of course. How much do you charge?"

They said it very innocently, and looked right at me, like they weren't asking for much. Like it was no big deal. Like my beloved faith was as hollow as their church and just as available. They were like pickpockets, these two, him distracting me while she slipped her tiny hand between my ribs and felt around for my soul.

Someone told them I was cool, so they thought I was the minister they were looking for.

God

Damn

Me

if I ever gave anyone that impression.

Their modern flippancy made me feel primitive. It brought back my old demons. At that moment I wished I could be anywhere but there, and anything but a minister. I felt them drawing me to the center, to the place of American Christianity, soft and uncommitted, enmeshed with culture, neither here nor there.

I wanted them to go somewhere, somewhere away. I wished they would move toward the cold clarity of unbelief or toward the throbbing heat of primitive religion. I wanted to reboot and call out to my pagan brothers and sisters. I wanted to howl like a Banshee with a wailing cry that would chill their bones and make them believe in the little people.

They made me so tired.

They were young, and they didn't know what they were asking. They really didn't, God love 'em. And how could they know? American Christianity has been marketed to death. It's been bundled with our culture and sold two-for-one on the discount table. Why should we be surprised when people show up at the hollow church, rummaging through our icons and using them to decorate their cakes.

We're the ones who put on the sale. We can't blame people when they come looking for bargains.

I tried to be nice in my refusal. "I'm sorry. I can't do what you're asking. I can't take God out of the wedding service. It would be a betrayal of my calling. I just . . . I'm not the minister you're looking for."

What they did next was the most disturbing thing of all. It was more saddening than walking into the hollow church. It was more depressing than when they asked me to deGod the service.

They huddled for a second, whispering to each other. Then they nodded, apparently coming to a decision. He spoke for the two of them. "That's cool. That's okay. You can leave all that stuff in — do the service however you like. We're fine either way, really. It's all good."

They really didn't care one way or the other. It absolutely did not matter to them at all.

The Preacher

George's story

George the Middle

This is the middle story in a trilogy of stories I wrote about my friend George. I began with the middle because it felt right. Later I thought about that and decided that it felt right to start in the middle because that's what my friendship with George was like. We dropped right into the middle of each other's lives. George was in the middle of dying, and I was in the middle of trying to figure out what kind of pastor I was going to be.

There is no way to plan for people like George. He doesn't fit in any easily defined categories, for one thing. When you meet someone like him, you just take what you can get and hang on for the ride.

I usually change the names of the people in my stories, but not this time. George is dead so I don't think he'll mind, and it feels real nice to be using his name again.

When George first came to our church, his T-cell count was at zero, and it seemed like AIDS had won the war. After he became a deacon in '97, he started the new Protease Inhibitor drugs, but it was too late for him. The treatment prolonged his life, but made him wish he were dead.

He started smoking marijuana again. It was the only thing that helped the pain. He had a ceramic water pipe shaped like a winged horse that he lovingly called "Pegasus." Most deacons don't hit the pipe, but George had need, and we kept it our little secret.

I remember the night George told me he was stopping the treatments. We were sitting in my yard, watching the stars, drinking beer, and praying. Well, George was praying. I was just drinking and listening. George liked to pray out loud and called God, "Dad." His own father had been a real asshole. The nicest thing he ever did was die young.

"It's just not worth it," he said. "I've reached the place where I want the pain to go away more than I want to live."

I cried a little, he waited for me to finish, and that was that. We spent some time planning his funeral and I took notes to make sure I would remember everything when the time came.

I had no idea how fast he would go down. That very Sunday he showed up for church in a wheelchair. During the service he felt something burning in his pants and tried to take them off. Dementia was starting to set in.

After that, coming to church was too hard for George, so we had a communion service at his home. Just a few people came, including Don, an ex-Pentecostal who had dropped that theology but kept his guitar and Jesus songs, and a fourth-grade girl with her mom.

Christians understand communion in different ways. For me, communion is the time to lay down everything that doesn't matter and celebrate the realization that you are not alone on this journey. It's a pretty important ritual for us.

We brought the wine, the bread, and Don's guitar to George's house. Don was about a third of the way through his Jesus songs when George started feeling the pain. He reached behind his chair, pulled out Pegasus, and proceeded to take two HUGE hits off that bad boy, complete with the classic *"hold it . . . hold it . . . exhale"* drama.

I've been in a lot of worship services, and I've seen some weird things happen. My own daughter blasted a huge fart during worship once and cracked up the whole church, but I'd never seen anyone whip out a bong right in the middle of communion.

No sir, I had not seen that.

I can promise you the good Christians with me on this mission of mercy had never seen it either. The Jesus music died, but not sudden-like. It kinda wound down like when you unplug a record player. I could see the little fourth-grader mouthing, "What's he doing, Mommy?"

I thought to myself, "Deacon George's lil' secret is out now!"

When George was done he put the pipe away and looked at us as if to say, "Why'd the music stop?"

It was Don who got things going again. He jumped right back into a Jesus song and the rest of the service went without a hitch. We all hugged George on the way out, and he seemed VERY much at peace.

Turns out that was the last time I would see the George that I remember. The next time I spoke with him he was in a coma.

*　　*　　*

My Christian tradition does not understand the elements of communion to be vehicles of grace. They are symbols and reminders of a great sacrifice and of just how much it costs to set things right.

I've thought a lot about our last service with George and about that third element he introduced into our communion worship that day. The sustaining breath from Pegasus was a reminder of our high calling to comfort those who stand in need.

"I will ask the Father and he will send the comforter to you, the very God-breath of truth."

Jesus said that.

George the Beginning

In 1996 an AIDS patient in our local hospital had a delirious vision. He was medicated and in deep pain when he saw Jesus standing by his bedside. The man's name was George.

At that very moment, a chaplain, who happened to be my wife, walked into the room.

George had left Christianity behind long ago, along with his dead father and a lot of other bad memories. He normally would have asked the chaplain to leave, but the vision shook him up a little, and he felt like talking to someone.

Over the next few days, George asked her some pretty tough questions. She said, "I know someone you might like to talk with."

That's how George and I ended up meeting at the Subway sandwich shop. All I knew was that a guy named George wanted to talk to me about God. All George knew was that I was a pastor who supposedly didn't mind questions.

By the time we met, George's Jesus vision had faded, and he was asking himself how the hell he got into this. Meeting ministers for lunch was not his idea of a good time.

He showed up ready to do battle. He hit me with his toughest questions and a lot of anger. Religion and abuse had gone hand-in-hand with his father, and he told me all about it. He was talking so fast I was starting to slip into a coma.

I'm not above a good fight, but I was so tired. I'd been fighting fundamentalist Christians for twenty years, had left my denomination, and had washed ashore with the only congregation that would have someone like me as their pastor. I didn't have any fight left in me.

So I said the first thing that came to my mind.

"Fuckin' A, man. Fu-Kin'-A."

I have found over the years that with some people, a well-placed "F-bomb" is the best pastoral move I can make. It's like a conversational "Ctrl-Alt-Delete." If nothing else works, just reboot and start over.

George, who had never heard a preacher say the "F-word," started to laugh. Then I started laughing too. We couldn't stop and the pimply-faced Subway guy thought we were out of our minds. I guess we were, kind of.

And so it began — a real live friendship. We discovered we had much in common. We both loved astronomy and movies and junior physics, having both read *Dancing Wu Li Masters* and Stephen Hawking, but nothing else. We both loved science fiction. George was hooked on sci-fi classics while I liked the zippy new stuff, but we agreed that *Foundation* kicked ass.

Mostly we shared a sense of humor and a way of looking at the world. George was a kindred spirit. You ever meet someone like that? It's amazing when it happens.

We always met at Subway. George was in very poor health, and for some reason their sandwiches didn't make him sick. We talked about life, and facing death, and AIDS, and God, and grief, and fathers, and every other thing you can imagine.

I sure do miss him.

One day George said, "I wish I could believe in God. I really do. I'd like to go to your church, and sing hymns, and be a part of something bigger than myself. I'm at the end of my life, and I don't think I've made a real difference in the world. My life hasn't really mattered to anyone. But, I just can't believe in God, so . . ."

You should never tell this preacher you don't believe in God.

"You don't believe in God? So what. Sometimes I don't either. The important question in life is not a question of belief. What's really important is whom you serve. I think it's serving God that makes life meaningful."

"You mean I could go to church, and sing, and do stuff, and all that, without believing in God?"

"Hell yes. I hope so, or else I better find another fuckin' job."

"You don't believe in God?"

"Well, I do now, mostly. I still have my bad days. It's complicated. Belief comes later for some people, for people like you and me."

"What would I do? How would I get started?"

"I don't know, I guess just come to church and sing."

Understand that this preacher NEVER asks people to become Christians. If anything, I warn people. I consider following Jesus to be a pretty stiff commitment, and I don't ever sugar coat it.

If someone is seeking a spiritual path and wants to journey with me, I'm fine with that. I'll shoulder my pack, help get his adjusted, and we'll move on down the road together. I don't really give a shit about making converts. That's not my business. I will walk with people though, if they want.

That's really all church is about anyway. We're a bunch of rag-tag pilgrims sharing the road and taking turns shielding each other from the wind. Sometimes we carry each other's packs for a spell. We share maps and provisions and friendship. We serve God by serving each other.

It ain't no big deal, and it is a big deal, if you know what I mean.

George came to church every Sunday after that. He just listened at first. Later he prayed some. He loved to sing. George was 5′6″ and weighed about 110 lbs., but he had the richest baritone voice you ever heard. Jesus, that guy could sing.

I wish you could see George the way I remember him. Black tennis shoes, faded jeans, and a flannel shirt with a tie. Sometimes suspenders too, I shit you not. Singing his heart out.

After awhile I noticed everyone wanted to sit near George so they could hear him sing. People stayed around after church to talk with him. He would sometimes stay late and help me put stuff away. That was George's spiritual program. Come. Listen. Sing. Pray. Help me put stuff away.

A visitor once grabbed me after church and said, "Who is that little man with the beautiful voice?"

"That's George."

"There's something almost saint-like about him."

"Yeah."

I don't know if it was because he was facing death, or because of all his new friends, or because God was working in his life, but there WAS something rather saint-like about George. It's hard to explain.

George did become a Christian. It just happened somewhere along the way. Somewhere along the way he made his peace with God. I'm not saying he always believed, but he made peace. I don't know when and I don't mark that kind of thing on the calendar. He found what he needed.

You want to call it belief? Go ahead. I call it more than belief. I call it faith.

I baptized him in a swimming pool. The whole church turned out for the party. We had BBQ. After George came up out of the water, a lot of folks jumped in and went swimming.

That was a good day.

About six months after George was baptized, we needed to elect a new deacon. At our church, deacons are servants. They have no power. They look after the sick, greet people, help put stuff away, that kind of thing.

I got a shock when I started reading the ballots.

George

George

George

George

George

When I called him to ask if he would be our deacon, he was stunned. "Why the hell did they vote for me? All I ever do is sing and talk to people and put stuff away."

"Exactly," I said.

He shook his head, trying to figure it out. "What does this mean?"

I thought for a minute and said, "I think, George, it means that you matter to these people. I think it means they see something good in you. I think it means George has made a real difference at our church."

And he was OUR deacon all the days of his life.

George the End

When George stopped taking his medicine, I knew it was only a matter of time, but I couldn't believe how fast it happened. In just a few days I got a phone call and was told George had fallen asleep and could not wake up. He was taken to a hospice facility to be made as comfortable as possible. We were told it wouldn't be long.

At that time our church had three deacons. JoAnn, a school nurse and mother of three; Tom, a high school band director; and George.

I called the other deacons, grabbed my portable CD player, and jumped in the car. When I arrived, JoAnn and Tom were already there. I saw a tiny stick figure lying on his left side under a thin sheet. He was so small and frail. JoAnn was leaning on the bed, stroking George's hair and talking to him. Tom was holding his hand and standing quietly by. The only noise coming from George was the mantra sound of labored breathing.

We waited for death with George. He never did respond to us, but we said a lot to him. We had all heard that dying people are aware of more than you think. We didn't know if this was true, but we talked to

George just in case it was. We took turns holding his hands and speaking softly into his ear. I don't remember how long we were there, but it seemed long.

Eventually we got tired. George seemed stable, so we decided to go home and return in the morning.

I placed my CD player on the pillow behind his head and put in "Singing with the Angels" by Darrell Adams. Darrell is a friend of mine who sings hymns with nothing but a guitar and a soul full of conviction. He also has one of the most angelic voices you've ever heard. Imagine Burl Ives as a whiskey drinking, Kentucky Baptist Democrat with fire in his eyes and a finger on the pulse of Jesus. Imagine that and you're close to understanding Darrell Adams.

George loved hymns so much that I figured Darrell's music would reach him if anything could. I set my player to repeat forever, and we left.

I got the call at 3:30 that morning. When I walked into the room, Darrell was still singing but George had gone away.

I never really got to say a formal goodbye because he died so suddenly. On the other hand, our whole friendship was one big goodbye.

I did George's funeral and tried my best to put his life and death into words. You can't ever do this, but knowing you can't, trying anyway, and keeping it short, is the best formula I've found for funerals.

About a week later I was given a cardboard box containing a few things that George left me. Pegasus was not in the box. I never found out what happened to him. George left me his beloved copy of *Stranger in a Strange Land* and a rock.

At that time our church owned a piece of land, but had no building. We were dreaming of a place of our own while meeting in schools, bars, fire stations, and anywhere else we could gather. George had picked up a rock during a prayer service on the land and kept it by his bed. He knew he would not live to see the building.

This was the rock he left me.

Two years after George died, we built a small church nestled among the live oak, mountain laurel, and native persimmon trees on a wild piece of property that we never intend to tame. It is a simple, stone building that suits us well. There is no pulpit or stage in our church. The main feature is a large fireplace with a mantle that is a huge beam from a 150-year-old Amish barn that was torn down.

During construction, I met the stonemason and gave him George's rock. He embedded it in the wall near the back door. I took a black marker and wrote "George's Rock" on it. I have to rewrite this about twice a year because the wind and the rain wear his name away.

I don't want George's name to go away. That's probably why I'm telling you this story.

Sometimes new people notice George's rock. If they ask about it, someone who knew him will tell them the story. We hope they come to understand that love is a deep and powerful force that can outlast death. Witness how George continues to touch lives.

We hope they see that God's best blessings are given to the world through people who have the courage to be faithful in small ways. George came, he sang, he talked to people, and he helped put things away.

This was the George that we knew. He was both the least and the greatest in the Kingdom of Heaven.

The Preacher

I'm sorry for what I said about the moon

I'm sorry for what I said about the moon that night when you and I were driving home from church. You were only five, and you had your face pressed against the window, watching the moon. I was only forty, and I had my mind pressed in upon itself, torqued and worried, racing and fretting and wholly out of touch with the present.

You were only in the present, only seeing and worshipping. You saw the beautiful roundness of the moon slipping behind trees and over the mall, silly and playful and keeping perfect pace with our car. The moon turned her mysterious attention upon you. She chose you out of thousands and said you were special. She was following us, and you rightly wanted to know why.

Dear heart, I gave you what I could that night, but I had to pull myself out of my thoughts and my adult world. It was like pulling a brush out of tangled hair, and it hurt a little. I wasn't at my best. I gave you an answer that was true but terribly false. I told you something that you need to know but shouldn't know. The thing I told you will dry you up and shut you down and seal up your eyes forever. I told you something that children ought not be told.

I was careless, and I'm sorry for what I said about the moon.

I said, "The moon isn't following us. It only looks like it's following us because . . ."

And then I was struck dumb. Maybe by the moon, I don't know. I tried to find a way to tell you that the distance from the earth to the moon is so great, relative to the distance we travel in cars, that the moon seems to stand outside the relative motion of the closer objects we see passing by the window when we drive.

That's the idea I had in my mind, but there's no way to say such a thing to a five-year-old. It won't fit into your primitive language. Perhaps we should never have fit it into ours.

I hesitated and was lost. I couldn't find any verbal purchase. Meaning and speech were like an owl gliding across a full moon. There was no holding anything that night.

She put quite a spell on us both, the moon did. That's what I think now.

So I had no answer for you. I should have left it at that, but I forced myself to speak anyway. I said, "I know your eyes are telling you that the moon is following us, but it isn't. I know it doesn't make sense to you right now, but you'll just have to trust me on this one."

You looked at me in that way that makes my love a little crazy. It makes me think my chest is going to start hurting if I don't get my arms around you. It's a quiet and thoughtful look with no expression. Just your eyes, innocent and wide through your bifocals, a little bigger than they should be. Processing, processing, processing. You wanted so to under-stand this deep mystery that was apparently locked in my adult head.

And then you looked back at the moon, who said nothing but moved with silent light, slipping behind the scary white tower as smoothly as a yolk in a black bowl. The moon answers no one. Time is on her side. Fa-thers who say she does not follow children will one day die, but the moon will always be here, steady and patient, outlasting all newfangled ways of seeing, taking all comers.

You were caught, weren't you? Caught between your love and your eyes. It won't be the last time, I'm afraid.

Everything in your heart tells you that I love you, and everything in your experience convinces you I am wise. And you know that I tell you the truth, even about big and little things.

Little Pea, I want to tell you that everything I said that night was true in its own way, God help us both.

But your eyes, your own eyes. They told you that the moon was fol-lowing us. Your very own eyes.

For a tortured moment you hung between the moon and your fa-ther, and then . . .

And then, I think you chose the moon. You broke eye contact slowly, like you could slip away without me noticing. You never doubted my sincerity, but you disagreed. And your exception was duly noted by all the powers. You left me and turned back to the moon, your mind racing a hundred miles and a thousand years in sweet, little-girl circles all the way home.

I saw you choose the moon, and I was proud of you. You chose the truth of your own eyes and still kept your love, and you were only five. I think you are a strong-minded young woman and a joy for this world.

I was not sorry for what I said about the moon that night. On that night I thought I said the right thing. But the moon, she never forgets. She caught me one year later on a cold, black morning. She chased me all the way to church and reminded me of what I said to you.

It was then that I became sorry for what I said about the moon.

This is what I say about the moon

The moon is patient. She bides everything, especially her time. She laughs at our petty sophistications. She knows she is deep under our skin. She has seen it all before.

You were safe in your little bed when I left for church in the wee hours of that Sunday morning, well before dawn. It was one year after I told you the moon does not follow little girls.

The cold was delicious. I sucked it in and blew it out. The stars were stark and clean the way they are in the early morning if the night air has chased away the clouds and the humidity. It was a moonish morning, you might say, and all the colors were muted and gray except for the yellow Bethlehem light that awaited my arrival at the church door.

I stopped beside my car to pay homage to the stars, as is my custom, for I am a magus at heart. And then I saw the moon.

A full moon in the hours before dawn carries a very old power. At least in my heart it does. And this moon, hanging above the houses, caught my eye.

"Look at YOU," I said.

I couldn't keep my eyes off her while I drove to church. She kept perfect pace off to the right, above the roofs. When I made my first turn, the moon slipped behind me like the Red Baron dropping out of the clouds. At the S-curve by the old farm, where you and I saw the raccoon, she bobbed and weaved, flitting from mirror to mirror to mirror and back again.

At one point she slid smoothly into my windshield and hung there, just to be playful. She said, "I know where you're going, and I'll already be there when you arrive."

I'm sorry to say that I was not afraid. I have moved beyond those good and old fears. But I wish I had been afraid, for I was going to the sacred place to pay homage to The Creator that morning, and this has become far too common a thing for me. A little fear would not have been a bad thing, I think.

But I was charmed, at least. My eyes were open to the beauty of the moon, and she followed me all the way to church. How could I deny it? When I left you in your bed she was with me, and when I arrived at church she was with me still. If this is not following, what does following mean?

I got out of my car with my Bible and my keys, and the moon was peeping at me through the ragged top of the juniper tree that leads to the dark woods behind the church. I looked at her, and she looked at me. I moved to the right and she followed, popping out from behind the juniper. I moved left and she did the same. Entranced, I moved right and left and right and left.

If anyone had come to our church at 5:47 am on that Sunday morning, they would have seen the minister, Bible in hand, dancing with the moon like any shaman or ancient priest of the oak groves.

Just like any other pagan.

The wind blew, and I felt the moon say, "Get thee inside, naughty boy. You know where you belong. You chose your way."

If memory serves, I was quick in my step and fumbling with my keys, heart racing, for the children of nature were nipping at my heels. Elves and fairies, brownies and tree spirits were running with the moon that nightly morning. All the wonderful old things of the world.

I opened the door and slipped inside, closing it firmly behind me. There before me were the quieter symbols that some say put to death the children of nature. There were cross and chalice and book of The Word.

But the cross is of rough, hewn wood and the chalice of fired clay. The book of The Word is all leaves and trees, and their ancient whisper can still be heard when the pages turn. Behold my kit and my tackle, the tools of this trade and calling. I took them up to make ready, but the moonlight shone on the stony floor through the window in the eternal moment before I turned on the light and shooed her away.

"Get thee outside, naughty girl. You know where you belong."

She left with a giggle and a splash but called out to me one last time.

"You aren't as sophisticated as you think, Man of The Word. Remember Mother Moon and Father Tree. Remember us with kindness, and show your respect for the old truths from which your new truth sprang. We are ever with you and always shining through your windows. Our old hopes live in your new.

"And one last thing. Do not ever say to a child that the moon does not follow her. Do not blaspheme or grieve the ancient spirits."

That is the moment when I became sorry for what I said about the moon. And I tell you that I was never more ready to proclaim the day of the Lord than I was on that day.

And so, little one, if you were to ask me again, I would tell you another truth. The moon follows every child who has not lost the ability to see. What omnipresence is this? What care? What patience of being? Now I say that nothing in all the world follows us with more beauty and grace than a full moon on a cold morning.

Never, my child. Never, ever close your eyes to the fullness of her presence or the beauty of her ancient mercies.

The Preacher

Call me Israel and I shall proclaim the day of the Lord

You cannot learn to preach in a classroom or by reading books. Preaching is a craft, so you must follow the way of the craftsman. It is a long and lonely journey. Do not be in a hurry, for it takes a good decade to settle in.

Your apprenticeship begins the first time you stand in the pulpit for the big event. That apprenticeship ends when you realize that Sunday morning isn't the big event at all, but is only the final act in a long week of good living. The delivery of the sermon is not the main point. When you learn this truth, you are ready to begin.

The preaching life is a pulmonary existence, a living made of inhaling and exhaling. There is a cadence to this life, a rising and falling. Lungs fill and are emptied. It is the very Spirit of God we seek, and it is interesting to me that the biblical words for "Spirit" are breathing words. The Hebrew word *Ruach* and the Greek word *Pneuma* are used to describe the Spirit of God, but they also mean "wind" or "breath."

If you want to preach well, forget about learning to speak. Speaking will come in its own time. You must learn to breathe.

There is a pressure that sits on the chest of a preacher. It comes from knowing he must have something to say come Sunday morning. Use this pressure like a bellows to get you breathing. Pull everything you can find into your lungs and let the sermon be your blessed exhalation. Live and breathe first, then study; speaking is last.

Breathe, damn you. Grab your text with both hands. Sink your feet into the earth. Think hard, read broad, breathe deep. Listen to God and to children. Let the sermon age in your earthen vessel. Do not open this cask until it has become fermented and heady. Then pop that cork and let it breathe.

On Friday draw your deepest breath. Receive everything you have found on your journey. Fill your lungs. On Sunday morning exhale. Be emptied. Be done. Be weak. On Monday, begin again.

There are no shortcuts to this process, at least none that will sustain you over the years. Shallow breathing tricks might work for a short time, but you have miles and years ahead of you.

This is the preaching life, and most weeks this is a life that I love. Most weeks I find breathing and living to be an absolute joy.

But there are other weeks. Weeks when my breathing is labored. Weeks when I am sad or lonely or depressed, and my lungs are clotted or collapsing. Weeks when I only want to take shallow breaths. Weeks when I do not believe in God, not if we define believing with any kind of living integrity.

These are the weeks when I do not want to stand up and be the Preacher. What kind of exhalation will I have if my lungs have been sucked empty, their walls sticking together like limp balloons. How will I speak if my vocal chords are starving for air, straining and dry?

Only there is a community of believers who count on me to proclaim the day of the Lord. They count on me to find hope in the scriptures. They believe in me and that matters more than whether or not I believe in myself.

Here is the truth that is so hard. If you are going to preach, you must believe what you have come to say. Lying is not an option. If you ever start lying from the pulpit your soul will wither on the vine, and that loss will become a depression so black that light cannot escape it. You will discover a singularity of sadness, sorrow compressed to a single point behind your eye.

Any two-bit hack can lie. Any con-artist can pretend to believe in his snake oil. You must never lie or pretend. You must believe your message, and you must proclaim it even in your darkest and loneliest weeks.

You must keep breathing.

Behold, the real preaching journey. Learning to breathe and believe in the hard weeks marks your coming of age as a proclaimer. For it is in these difficult weeks that you learn the deep secrets of faith, indeed the very meaning of the word. In the saddest times your soul must take its deepest breaths, stretching itself and opening deep channels for the Spirit of God.

No one can tell you how to keep believing in the middle of a faithless week. You must find your own way, pilgrim. I can give you a few hints to get you started. You will need to become ferocious and large. You will need to hold onto God and refuse to let go until you receive your blessing. It is a lungful you need and failure is not an option. You must demand and you will receive.

You must also be ready to live with whatever dislocation comes from meeting The Creator hip to hip. It will be a jarring blow and you may limp thereafter.

Study hard. Breathe deep and hear your prayers. Cut a fresh covenant and hang onto God with two hands and both eyes shut. Don't worry if your feet leave the ground. Never let go until you have what you need.

Do whatever it takes, but do be ready. You are the preacher, and someone must proclaim this day.

Here is a prayer that might help.

"I speak to The One who created and is able to hold galaxies and children in his hands. I am a weak and small man. I will need your help if I am to speak the truth. Let my preaching invite and empower. Let your people walk with me as I limp after the Good Shepherd along a very narrow way.

"Make me bold without being proud. Help me be passionate without drawing attention to myself. Let me lead and follow at the same time. Show me how to be weak and strong, simple and deep. Breathe in me and bring my clay to life. Fill my lungs with a double portion of your Spirit.

"I mean no disrespect, but I am not leaving until you bless me with The Word.

"Call me Israel, and I shall proclaim the day of the Lord."

The Preacher

What if

What if we suddenly saw the world with God's eyes? What if the reality of good and evil exploded into our consciousness in a blinding flash of inspiration?

What if this happened right in the middle of church?

Would we fall out of our pews, bawling at our first glimpse of real beauty? Would there be a mad rush for the exits, everyone scrambling to enter the real cathedral? Would goodness burst our fragile hearts?

And if, in that same instant, the stark reality of evil became clear, what would happen to us? What if we saw the face of an abused child at the very apex of her suffering? What if we suddenly bore the knowledge of every child's pain? What if we understood the exponential evil that grows from our sterile apathy?

Would we become like animals, howling our mourning instead of singing our hymns? Would our Bibles, psalters, and hymnbooks become as dead wood in our hands? Would we throw them to the ground and tear across the face of creation, rushing to the rescue of one child in the name of all that is holy?

Would we then turn on our church buildings in a mad rage, tearing them to the ground like Ents ripping at Orthanc? Would our righteous anger and sorrow for years of misplaced energy prove to be an elemental force destroying every remnant of what we once called Church?

And what if the people of our world beheld such lunatics, possessed of an unspeakable Spirit?

What would they think?

But we are not that people. We are not able to bear that burden. We are not ready for the fruit of the tree of the knowledge of good and evil.

We are only men and women, singing hymns, murmuring prayers, trying to cover our nakedness.

The Preacher

Do this in remembrance of me

When I first began Real Live Preacher, the Salon bloggers were very helpful and encouraging. I made some nice friendships, but none more unexpected than my friendship with Hugh Elliott. Hugh writes the Salon blog called "Standing Room Only." In the very early days of Real Live Preacher, Hugh sent encouraging emails and even helped me figure out how the blogging software worked.

In time, what began as kindness blossomed into a real live friendship.

All of this is very surprising if you consider the fact that Hugh Elliott had more reason to be suspicious of me than anyone else. Hugh is a gay man with AIDS who lives in Los Angeles. Like many homosexuals, Hugh has experienced the darkest side of Christianity. It is still amazing to me that Hugh was willing to read my writing and send emails to a man who called himself "Real Live Preacher."

I am grateful for his willingness to make himself vulnerable and hope that someday I get to meet Hugh in person.

Part 1

At some point in this story, reality turns to fantasy. I wish I could tell you exactly when that happens, but I'm not sure myself.

I received a religious catalog in the mail. I never in a thousand million years asked for it. Thumbing through this thing was surreal. Page after page of smiling models in clerical robes, battery-powered candles with fake dripping wax, and communion wafers by the case.

Autom Wafers starting at $8.95 a box
20% thicker
No crumble design
25% more wheat

There was even a spooky, snap-together communion table made of Plexiglas, looking like something out of a 1960s science fiction movie. The machine-etched "This Do in Remembrance of Me" seemed too sterile for a man's last request.

I didn't like the pictures this catalog was bringing to my mind.

Somewhere there is a woman sitting in a factory before an endless line of communion chalices. Her vacant expression of despair is reflected in the silver cups as they pass in front of her. Her image jumps a little as each engraved Chi Rho goes by.

Somewhere there is a man operating a communion wafer machine, stamping out perfect, round wafers, one after another. Kachunk, Kachunk, Kachunk. Mr. Rogers never visited THIS factory.

Do you think anyone ever lost a hand in the wafer press? Was real flesh and blood ever a part of this process?

The catalog slipped from my hand and fell to the floor. I closed my eyes. I was getting that old, familiar feeling of disorientation and despair.

And then HE started talking.

I don't know who he is, but he always shows up at just the right moment. Jung knew. So did Mick Jagger. His is a dark voice, oily and smooth, bubbling up crude from the bottom of your soul.

"Pleased to meet you. Hope you guess my name."

"Hey there, Preacher. Long time no see. When did YOU start wearing a collar? Denim. Nice. I didn't know they had those. When was the last time we talked, anyway?"

"I think it was when Tom gave me the key."

"No kidding? That WAS a long time ago. That was hilarious, by the way. You, sitting there asking God if he really thought you ought to be a pastor, and a gay man walks up and gives you a key to his church. What was it he said?"

"He said they wanted me to come and go as I pleased."

"Oh yeah. Outstanding. A homosexual made room for YOU at church. Maybe it's just me, but I think that's some funny shit. Have you told THEM about it?"

"Told who about it?"

"Whom! The blog people. The ones who are reading this right now."

"No. I think I'll keep Tom's story for myself."

"Whatever. So why'd you call me?"

"I didn't call you."

"Sure you did. You always do, but let's not argue about that. What's that you're reading?"

"It's just this stupid catalog thing. I don't know where it came from."

"Let me see. Oh yeah, I love this one. Such deliciously bad taste. Sam Walton meets Jerry Falwell. Wanna sit around and make fun of it?"

"No."

"What's a matter, you depressed again?"

"No. Yeah. I guess so. It's this damn catalog. Something's wrong with it, with THIS." I shook it vigorously.

He looked at me for a long moment, and then a little smile started to sneak onto his face. It grew until he lost control and burst into laughter.

"Oh sweet Jesus. C'mon, you gotta be kiddin' me, right? There's a bazillion churches in this country. There must be a hundred thousand communion tables in South Texas alone. Robes, candle stands, crosses, pews. Where do you think all that stuff comes from? If you're going to have churches, you're going to have to have places that make and sell church stuff.

"What, did you think communion bread was baked by little old ladies and delivered in baskets with red-checkered napkins?

"You're such a jackass. There's nothing wrong with that catalog. Church is big business in this country, and it's all handled professionally. Anyway, I don't know why you got YOUR panties in a wad. You ain't so innocent yourself."

"Whatta you mean?"

"Christ almighty, I'm not going to spell it out for you. This isn't some made-for-TV movie. You're not some fresh, young Kentucky Fried Chicken executive, fainting at his first sight of the chicken farm. You knew church was big business. Hell, you're a professional minister. Where do you think your paycheck comes from, dipshit?

"There's nothing more corporate than that computer-generated paycheck you get. I don't see you whining when you cash it."

He was right. I'd been hearing this voice for ten years. I always knew he was right, but the catalog broke something in me. I took off my collar and laid it on my desk. He laughed while I slid my church key off my key ring.

"You've GOT to be kidding me. Like you're going to quit right now. What are you gonna do for money? You don't have any skills. Are you gonna flip burgers? You gonna sell used cars?"

He snickered. "Actually, you'd make a damn good used car salesman.

"Hey, I know. Why don't you put a PayPal button on Real Live Preacher? Maybe some of your readers will send you a buck or two. Course you won't be a real live preacher if you leave that collar on the table. And we both know you won't really lay that collar down."

"And anyway, if you aren't going to be a real live preacher, who will you be, huh? I'll tell you who you'll be. Nobody."

I put my key and Bible on the desk with the collar and headed for the door.

"I'm going to see Hugh."

"What?"

"I'm going to Los Angeles. And I'm going to find Hugh."

"Hugh Elliott? The six-foot whatever gay guy who does 'Standing Room Only?'"

"Yes."

"You're going to drive all the way to Los Angeles, find his address in the phone book, and show up at Hugh Elliott's door? That's your big plan? That's what you're going to do?"

"Yes."

He doubled over, laughing uncontrollably. Between giggles, he managed to get out a few words.

"You know he doesn't want to see you, right? You do know that."

I stopped at the door and turned around. "Yes he does. He does want to see me. Hugh's the only one in the blog world who knows who I really am. Hugh Elliott is my friend."

"No, he's not. Look, you can be idealistic and silly and all that. It's sweet.

No really, I like that about you. But don't fool yourself. Hugh Elliott knows Real Live Preacher. That's all anyone knows. They like to read you, but they really don't want to know you. They certainly don't want you showing up at their doors looking for answers."

"You're a liar. I'm going to find Hugh."

"Okay, okay. You're going on a romantic little quest. Fine. Just answer me this: What are you going to say to him when you find him."

"I'm going to ask him to help me learn how to live. I'm not going to be a preacher anymore."

He was silent, and real fear flashed in his eyes for a moment.

I didn't wait for a reply. I walked out the door and away from the church. He stayed inside, but I could hear his final words through the stained glass.

"Watch his eyes when he answers the door and realizes it's you. Then you'll know he doesn't want to see you.

"His eyes will tell you the truth."

Part 2

I met Hugh Elliott, the man who writes "Standing Room Only," by email back in December of 2002 when I began Real Live Preacher. Hugh sent encouraging messages and helped me get started as a blogger. We've communicated regularly since then, and I consider him to be a real friend.

When Hugh suddenly stopped writing during a time of grief and loss, a number of bloggers were concerned about him, including me. On a crazy whim I sent him my name, address, and phone number. I told him to call me if he ever needed to talk.

So much for anonymity.

His own support systems bore the load, so he never needed to call, but for a long time Hugh was the only person in the blog world who knew who I was. A handful of people knew my first name, but he knew everything.

Okay, now you know about Hugh. Fast-forward to last week.

I got that crappy church catalog in the mail. Thumbing through it kicked up the disillusionment and depression that is always lurking just below my surface. It seemed to me that the church was nothing more than an institution. It seemed to me that the memory of Christ was very far away.

Sometimes when I'm down, I imagine what my life would be like if I just walked away from the church. When this happens, it does seem like a voice speaking to me. I think the voice is just me working through my sadness, but I don't claim any expertise in this.

On this day, Hugh Elliott came to mind. I thought I would like to stand toe-to-toe with Hugh and talk about what it means to live. In that crazy moment I sat down and started writing a story about the catalog and the voice and the promise of an upcoming fantasy visit to Los Angeles.

Of course, when you say you're going to write part two of a story, you need to honor that commitment.

Friday came and writer's block was setting in. I had to create a whole journey to Los Angeles, and the only thing I had written down was a snippet of dialogue that would take place when Hugh answered the door.

Me: *"I thought you'd be wearing a kimono or something."*

Hugh: *"Oh my God!"*

[pause]

Hugh: *"You think all gay men wear kimonos, don't you?"*

Friday night I was at home with my family, but half my brain was wondering what the hell I was going to write. I liked my little kimono bit, but it wasn't much to go on.

And then the phone rang.

It was a man, but I didn't recognize the voice. He said, "Do you know who this is?" I admitted that I didn't.

He laughed and said, "It's Hugh Elliott."

I shit you not.

We talked about everything, and we talked for a long time. We talked about my disillusionment and the bad table and the communion wafers by the box. It was wonderful.

The conversation ended like this:

"Well, if I ever decide to take off this collar for good, I'll come and see you, just like I said in that thing I wrote."

"That's not going to happen. You're not going to take off that collar."

"Why not?"

"Because I wouldn't let you."

"You wouldn't?"

"No. You've been called, and you have important work to do. Keep the collar. If you came to see me, I'd teach you to make bread."

There were a few more words, then we said goodbye. I didn't need to go to Los Angeles. Hugh came to me.

I gave him my phone number in case he needed me. He used it because he could tell I needed him. Hugh Elliott became my communion bread on Friday night. He became that vehicle of grace.

And I learned something in all of this that will help me the next time I let myself get depressed over something as silly as a bad religious catalog.

If the wafers are going stale for you, be the bread yourself. Break yourself open and nourish the world.

If the communion table seems cheap and tacky, become a table yourself. Be a resting place for the weary.

If you feel there are no more angels, pick up the phone and spread your own tidings.

Gather your bread. Set your table. Shout your good news.

Do these things in remembrance of HIM.

The Preacher

James, John, and Crazy Joe

RLPDV

It happened in one of those quiet moments when nothing much was going on. Peter whistled while he mended a net. Bartholomew picked at his sandal. The other guys were talking in small groups.

Jesus was sitting apart, looking north up the Jordan River. He was wondering about the man who used to live in the tombs on the south shore of the Sea of Galilee. The people around there used to call him "Crazy Joe."

After Jesus healed him, Crazy Joe wanted to join up. He wanted to become a disciple and go with them in the boat, but Jesus made him stay and make peace with his own people.

"Stay here and tell everyone what God has done for you."

It was the right thing to say and do, but he couldn't get Crazy Joe out of his mind. As they sailed away, Jesus was the only one who looked back. Crazy Joe was standing on the shore with his right hand out, as if he was still hoping to touch Jesus. He got smaller and smaller, but he never put his hand down.

James and John slipped away from the others and approached Jesus. "Teacher, will you do us a favor?"

"Um, maybe. What kind of favor?"

"Okay, well, uh . . . John and I, we know that you're going to have your own kingdom here pretty soon. We've heard you talking about it. When that happens, we'd like seats of honor, you know, at your right and left side."

James licked his lips nervously and glanced at John, who nodded his approval and then spoke up himself.

"Yeah, that's what we want. Seats of honor for the Sons of Thunder, you might say. I mean, we're always there for you, right? Right?"

Jesus didn't reply, but John didn't seem to notice.

"So anyway, we just want to be right there with you when you come into your own."

Jesus smiled. It was impossible to be angry at such a childlike request.

"Hmm. Interesting favor. Walk with me."

They moved a few steps farther away from the others, and then Jesus stood face-to-face with both of them.

"You don't know what you're asking. I'm not angry with you for telling me what you really want, but you can't possibly know what it is that you have asked. Do you think you are able to drink from my cup, the one that will be given to me in Jerusalem? Are you ready for that dose? Do you think you are ready for the baptism I will receive there?"

For a moment James and John were silent, as if they were really hearing him, but then they puffed out their chests and put on a look of bold confidence. James spoke for the two of them, with John nodding.

"Absolutely, Jesus. No problem. Whatever you need, you got it. We'll always be there for you."

That last phrase echoed over and over in his mind with the voices of a thousand people. "Always be there for you. Always be there for you. Always be there. Always be there."

That's what people promise, and that's what people want. "I'll always be there for you," and "Please always be there for me."

He looked north again, up the Jordan. That's what Crazy Joe wanted. He wanted to be with Jesus for always. He turned him down, and now Crazy Joe's voice haunted him. "Tell them the truth, even if it hurts. You told me the truth. Remember?"

Jesus looked at the two men facing him and loved them. He lifted his hands, cupping them over the place where neck meets shoulder. They imitated his embrace, and the three of them made a little triangle of arms and faces.

"Listen to me now. You WILL drink from my cup and you WILL receive my baptism. In time, both of these will come to you."

James and John grinned and looked pleased; Jesus groaned.

"Don't smile. You . . . Look, one day you will come to understand what my cup and baptism are. And on that day . . . Well, on that day I'll make sure you have what you need. I won't be there, but you won't be alone."

The Sons of Thunder both nodded, then James spoke. "So, what about those seats of honor? I appreciate all that stuff about sharing your cup and whatnot, but we were mostly interested in the seats."

"Yeah," John said. "What about those seats?"

Jesus laughed. It was a relief to move to a lighter subject. "Oh yeah, the seats of honor for the Sons of Thunder. You wanted the best seats in the house. Bad news, boys. I'm not in charge of the seating arrangements. Those seats are already reserved — have been for quite some time."

Peter's deep, bellowing voice startled them all. They had not been aware that he had walked up and heard the end of their conversation.

"Jesus, what the hell's going on here? Tell me I'm hearing things, cause it sounds like these two assholes are trying to get the best seats in your kingdom."

Peter told the others what he had heard, and the quiet conversation of three friends turned into a squabbling mess of angry men. Jesus sighed and then waded into the middle of it all.

"Stop it! Dammit, stop everything. Sit down! Peter, sit your ass down. Maybe I should have taken Crazy Joe and left the lot of you back there on the south shore."

He pointed at them. "See? You see? This is exactly what I DON'T want. I don't want you fighting over positions of power. I don't want you arguing about who is better. Can't you see how . . . ridiculous that is when we are surrounded by God's Spirit and his love? I don't want it to be like this. I want . . . I want . . ."

His voice trailed off and he stood staring. He saw Crazy Joe, this time back in the tombs, clothed and in his right mind. Crazy Joe, sitting by a grave, telling a woman who used to be afraid of him about the day Jesus changed everything.

Thaddaeus spoke up. "Um, what DO you want?"

Jesus turned and looked at them, his eyes making contact with each. "I want the greatest of you to be marked not by power, but by service. I want you to be backwards and upside down. I want you to be big by being small, rich by being poor. I want you to gain your lives by giving them away.

"I want you to be like Crazy Joe, having nothing but your story and needing only that. I won't always be here, you see. I won't and yet I will. When I'm gone and you aren't sure what to do, just tell your story.

"Just be small in the world and tell everyone what God has done for you."

Postscript

The book of Acts tells us that James was the first of the twelve to die in the name of Christ. Church tradition holds that John outlived all the other disciples and died as one of the last living links to Jesus.

Their deaths framed the apostolic period. One received the baptism of death and the other the cup of leadership.

Biblical References:
The story of James and John's big request, Mark 10:35-45
The story of "Crazy Joe," Mark 5:1-20
The Sons of Thunder, Mark 3:16-17
The death of James, Acts 12:1-2

The Preacher

One good thing

I listened. I watched. I go to this meeting every year, but this year I have new eyes. I don't know where I got these eyes, but I have them. And this year I see clearly.

I think I know what's going on here.

I didn't like sitting in the huge hall hearing sermons and speeches and watching video presentations and reviewing complicated budgets. My college roommate and seminary buddy Bruce saw me in the back. We sat together, bored out of our skulls. Bruce decided to write letters to some parishioners, occasionally nodding or clapping when everyone else did.

I'm writing this from behind a curtain, in a convention center, in a city here in Texas. I came to this place to attend a meeting for the leaders of our denomination. I couldn't take what I was hearing, so I stole out of the convention room, got a Diet Coke and some Nacho Cheese Doritos, found a quiet place, and decided to write instead.

I told you Jeanene and I were getting away for a couple of days. I just didn't mention that we were going to a religious meeting.

I know; it sounds pretty boring to me too. But we did get away without the kids, and we do have our own motel room.

Talk about your revival!

A group of church people decide they want to do good things in the name of Jesus. A few churches join forces, and they get some good things done. They do. Then someone asks this question: If doing a few good things in Christ's name is wonderful, how much better would a hundred good things be? How about a thousand?

Of course, if you mean to do a thousand good things for Jesus, you better get organized. You're going to need a lot of people and a lot of money.

The organization of people who want to do a lot of good things for Jesus grows until it can only be run by professionals and insiders who operate in a very tight, "good old boy" network. A person could make a career just learning how to negotiate this network, learning which hands to shake and which votes really matter. Soon, regular church people cannot comprehend the complexity of the organization, but they foot the bill for it. In an effort to keep the money coming, the insiders turn more and more of their efforts toward marketing the organization to their own people.

The goal is a magical balance. You want the lay people to be impressed enough to send money, but you want them intimidated enough to stay out of the way. It's good if you can flash a lot of Ph.D.'s and some unthinkably complex flow-charts.

What you end up with is millions of people paying thousands of people to manage the doing of good things for Jesus.

"Let us take care of things for you, sweethearts. Don't worry your pretty little heads, but do keep sending your money because we did 125,247 good things for Jesus last year, the highlights of which can be seen on our sixteen-minute video promo. With your help, next year will be even better, praise the Lord. Next year we might do over 150,000 good things for Jesus."

And that, my friends, is what we in the business call a denomination.

I made it through two hours of the first meeting, and then I couldn't stand it anymore.

I dropped my reports and pamphlets on the floor, picked up my complimentary tote bag, and left the big room. It was like leaving a ballgame to go to the bathroom. "Excuse me, excuse me, I'm sorry, excuse me." Then I was out. Out of there. Out of the big room. I wandered around, dazed, until I found a little place behind a curtain where I could pull out my computer and write this to you.

It's not that they don't do good things. They do. This particular organization has given homes and college educations to thousands of homeless children over the last twenty-five years, for example. It's not that I think I'm better than the people in this organization. Jesus, I'm not fit to kiss their feet. They are wonderful people as individuals, and I love them.

I think the problem is that the idea of spending a lot of energy supporting, marketing, and hyping a giant organization for the purpose of doing a bazillion good things for Jesus has lost its appeal for me. I can't wrap my mind around the idea of it. I don't think you can count good things done for Jesus and squeeze them onto a video tape. I don't understand the boundaries, I guess. I don't even know where a good thing for Jesus ends and just a plain old good thing begins.

I think — and I'm just talking here, just talking behind a little curtain, just wondering and asking — I think maybe I'd like to do just ONE good thing for Jesus. You know, just one good thing and give myself completely to it. And when I was finished doing my one good thing, I would have seen it through to the end, and I would know that it was a good thing I did. And then I could do another good thing for Jesus if I wanted to.

And I have a feeling that if I was completely engaged in my one good thing, I wouldn't have the time or energy to put into the organization for doing a million good things for Jesus. I'm sure they'll be fine without me. They seem to have a lot of inertia.

I wonder what would happen if everyone found one good thing to do in this world. I'm talking about regular people now, people like you and me. If we quit managing thousands of good things and did one good thing at a time, I think we would know the joy of work and the pleasure of rest. We would know the rhythm of week and Sabbath, of work and play, of night and day.

And if all of us were doing one good thing, wouldn't that add up to millions of good things?

And isn't that what we said we wanted all along?

The Preacher

Bringing Esau home

Like Isaac, did you wonder where this strange voice came from? Was this not the boy you held and wrestled and played catch with, marveling at his strong arm and growing muscles?

The body was that of Esau, but it was the voice of Jacob you heard. Jacob, smooth and slick. Jacob with his own plans and hidden agendas. Jacob, desperately needing to be blessed but knowing nothing of blessings.

Like Isaac, you trusted the body and ignored the voice. You drew me close, son to father, and you blessed me with the sacred words of our tradition and way.

What we both remember is that I came home from college, my head addled with a shiny new education and my heart bursting with a young man's passion for Christ. I came into the modest home where I was nurtured and before the father who raised me and said some young and foolish things. God forgive me, I said that I could never live like you lived, with a nice house and all the comforts of home.

"Following Christ means leaving all this behind," I said. "This is fine for you and Mom, I guess, but I can't live like this."

I said these things never thinking how they would hurt you. You who loved Christ enough to spend your whole life on the border and in between. You stood between your East Texas culture and its horrible racism. You stood between the expectations of your family and the way of Christ. You stood on the border between the poverty of Juarez and life as we knew it in El Paso.

I have come to understand that loves meets flesh on the border and in between. And love that never meets flesh is no kind of love at all. Love must have incarnation.

I loved the poor in some abstract sense, but you helped poor people. I had a theology, but you knew what it meant to whisper God words gently into the ears of the hurting. I cared about my image, but you cared about truth and about me.

You listened to me carefully and took me seriously. You shrugged off the sting of my words and looked behind them to my passion. You bore the pain and thought only of me.

And you said, "I'm so glad that you are taking seriously the call of Christ in your life. So very glad."

It took me fifteen years and having children of my own to understand what you gave me on that day. I have my own home now and my own family. I want to tell you that I still carry that blessing with me. I feel its power growing in my heart, and I hope to pass it on to my daughters when it is their time.

I have dreamed dreams and wrestled an angel or two. Keep the fire burning downstairs for me, for I am ready to cross the river and come home. I met Esau on the way and we are reconciled.

I'm bringing him home for Christmas this year.

The Preacher

Tetragrammaton

I recently watched *The Believer,* a movie based on the true story of Daniel Burros, a Jewish man who was a member of the American Nazi party in the 1960s.

I had such mixed emotions while watching it. I was horrified by such an intimate glimpse into the mind of an anti-Semite, but I was also deeply moved, even to tears.

The Believer gave voice to my own conflicted and troubled feelings about religion and the practice of faith in God.

Danny desecrates a synagogue with his neo-Nazi friends. He seems to be enjoying himself until one of the thugs cracks open the sacred Ark of the Law and casts the Torah scroll down onto the floor. It unrolls obscenely, the rich, white parchment revealing the precious hand-lettering inside.

This scene is so much like a rape that I sat forward in my chair and whispered, "No!"

When one of them tramples on the Torah with his dirty shoe, tearing the paper, Danny can no longer hide his grief. He rushes over and rescues the scroll, to the great confusion of his Nazi friends. He takes the Torah home, repairs it, and hides it in his closet.

This is the point in the movie when my feelings turned from horror to understanding. I am conflicted and ashamed, much like Danny. I understand his deep-seated conflict. I understand what it means to be stretched by forces pulling from opposite directions.

A woman in the movie told a classic Jewish joke. It seems a Jewish man was stranded on an island for many years. His rescuers found that he had built two synagogues on the island. They asked him why he had two, and he said, "One to pray in and the other not to step foot in for the rest of my life, so help me GOD."

I absolutely understand that joke.

I am an unbeliever at heart, you see. I can't help myself. Perhaps I'm not wired for belief, or maybe my wires are crossed. I just cannot bring myself to believe what I cannot see. This is who I am.

There is something wonderfully attractive about empiricism, something clean and crisp. God, to have such a clear boundary. Lord, to have an epistemology I could write on my thumbnail.

The universe seems wondrous to me, with or without God. It has powerful lines and uncompromising ways. Patience and time sit like sages on the planets, strong and impersonal. There is a stark beauty to all of this.

The coldness of empty space and the finality of death do not frighten me. Truth is the siren song that tugs at my weak heart. I bind myself to the mast with a phylactery.

I am so close to unbelief. So close that my faith has always been raw, like a wound that never heals. This flesh is ever red and tender, and I am drawn to lick it with my sandpaper cat tongue.

Just a duck and a sidestep, and I would be lost in the crowd, moving in a different lane and away to a new destination.

Just a duck
   and a sidestep.

And yet.

And yet.

And yet my hands long to run themselves over that scroll. I want to touch the paper and see if I can feel the energy of the calligrapher. Behold, the Tetragrammaton, the four letters, the name of God. How my heart beats faster at the very thought of THEE.

יהוה

My mind works from left to right, but the name of God fights against the flow of my thought, pushing rudely from right to left, elbowing its way into my heart.

There are no vowels in this word because this word IS vowel and needs no pointing. It is four hard consonant sounds, each followed by a burst of spirit wind, whatever you can summon. No living human knows for sure how this word was pronounced because the Jewish people stopped saying it, out of reverence, roughly 1,700 years old.

Hard sounds and the rush of your spirit. That's all we know.

I wonder. If I managed to speak this name properly, would there be anything left of me?

When I see the name of God, my eyes close and I groan in protest. It's like being seduced. My head says no, but my heart says, "Oh God, yes." My hands must touch the letters. I must smell the rich paper of the scroll. I must breathe and I must pray.

I give in. Again.

And so faith is closing your eyes and following the breath of your soul down to the bottom of life, where existence and nonexistence have merged into irrelevance. All that matters is the little part you play in the vast drama. All that counts is the obedience that marks the life you have been given.

The Preacher

Let him be called Real Live Preacher

November 2002
Somewhere in Heaven

One more thing, Excellency. A minor thing. You see it there at the bottom of your list. It's the question of what's to be done with Gordon Atkinson.

Gordon Atkinson? That name is not familiar to me.

It wouldn't be, my Lord. He's not particularly important, as it were, but of course that sort of thing has never mattered to Our Father. At any rate, he IS on your list.

Yes . . . well, tell me about him.

Not much to tell, really. He's a youngish man, early forties. Lives in a rather rugged part of Texas. And likes it, so the report says.

Ugh.

In any case, he lives there, and he is seeking to do the Father's work.

What sort of a man is he?

He's very worldly, my Lord. He spent his adolescent years playing sports, sneaking peaks at *Playboy,* listening to rock music, and watching violent movies. He has a morbid curiosity, I'm afraid. He's outspoken, weak at times, quick to judge, a bit lazy with the details, a procrastinator.

And he's vulgar.

Vulgar?

Terribly vulgar, my Lord. He's quite an embarrassment. We're not sure what to do with him.

Go on.

He's a fleshly man. A man who loves sensations. Hot food, cold drink, sex, that sort of thing. He spits. He breaks wind — loudly I might add. He belches. And he laughs at all of those things. He loves the earth and the body and all the usual sins that go along with persons of this sort.

Is there nothing GOOD you can tell me about this man?

There is SOME good, of course. He is a child of Our Father.

It hardly seems likely.

Yes. In any case, he's got an uncommon imagination and a streak of creativity to boot. His passion seems to match his vulgarity, as is often the case. He loves deeply and completely; I'll say that much for him. He's got an excellent sense of humor and a robust laugh. Hmm. This is interesting.

What?

Well, his file states clearly that his love and devotion to The Lord are complete and unquestioned. But it also says he isn't sure that God exists.

Bit odd, wouldn't you say?

There have been such cases, but yes, it is unusual.

I begin to get the picture.

One last thing, Excellency. He has a gift with words, spoken and especially written.

Does he know of this gift?

Well, he's been blathering on for a decade or so. He IS a preacher.

Good Lord, how did that happen?

Ah, unknown as of yet. We're making inquiries.

Have Simpkins from acquisitions sacked immediately.

It shall be done. Now, back to the question of Mr. Atkinson. He HAS been dabbling in writing for some time, and he's very keen on doing more of it. I recommend we encourage him, if only for this: it keeps him from watching reruns of *The Simpsons* at night, a ghastly waste of time to my way of thinking.

The Simpsons, eh? I have decided. He shall be a writer. But first, shoot him through with a white-hot bolt of fear, running from uvula to colon. Fear, understand? I want that colon to seize with it.

Fear, Excellency?

Yes. He deserves it. He won't mind, in any case. Simple fool will probably think it gives his writing an edge.

What shall he be afraid of, my Lord?

He shall be afraid of losing his soul, because he may well lose it. Make no mistake, we're taking a real risk with this character.

Agreed.

Then I'd like you to set him down in a lowly place. Somewhere out of the way. Let fear and love drive him, alternatively. Have you heard of weblogs?

No, my Lord. I don't get out much.

The boys in research will fill you in on the particulars. Make him a blogger, and let him stand by the door to the heavens, welcoming strangers. Perhaps someday he shall enter that door himself.

All shall be done as you have commanded.

Anything else, my Lord?

Just one more thing. Let him be called "Real Live Preacher."

It amuses me.

The Preacher